W.L. WILMSHURST

THE CEREMONY OF INITIATION

REVISITED BY

ROBERT LOMAS

About the authors

Walter Leslie Wilmshurst was born 22 June 1867 in Sussex. Seventy-two years later, on 19 July 1939, he was hailing a taxi in North London when he collapsed in the street and died, leaving behind him an incredible legacy from his fifty years as a Freemason. In between he spent his entire working life as a solicitor in Huddersfield, West Yorkshire. Brother Wilmshurst was a Freemason of his time and didn't speak of his Masonry outside the Lodge. Yet he thought deeply about it and shared his thoughts. He wrote lectures to deliver to his lodge, created private teaching materials to help his junior brethren, held discussions in Lodges of Instruction and kept detailed notebooks of his thoughts. He also wrote many classic books on Freemasonry, including *The Meaning of Masonry*, *The Masonic Initiation*, *The Ceremony of Initiation* and *The Ceremony of Passing*

Dr Robert Lomas has worked on cruise-missile guidance systems and Fire Brigade command-and-control systems and was involved in the early development of personal computers. He currently lectures in Information Systems at Bradford University School of Management. He is author, or co-author, of best-selling books on Freemasonry and Science, including *The Hiram Key*, *Turning the Hiram Key*, *Freemasonry and the Birth of Modern Science*, *The Man Who Invented the Twentieth Century* and *The Lewis Guide to Masonic Symbols*.

www.robertlomas.com   twitter: @Dr_Robert_Lomas

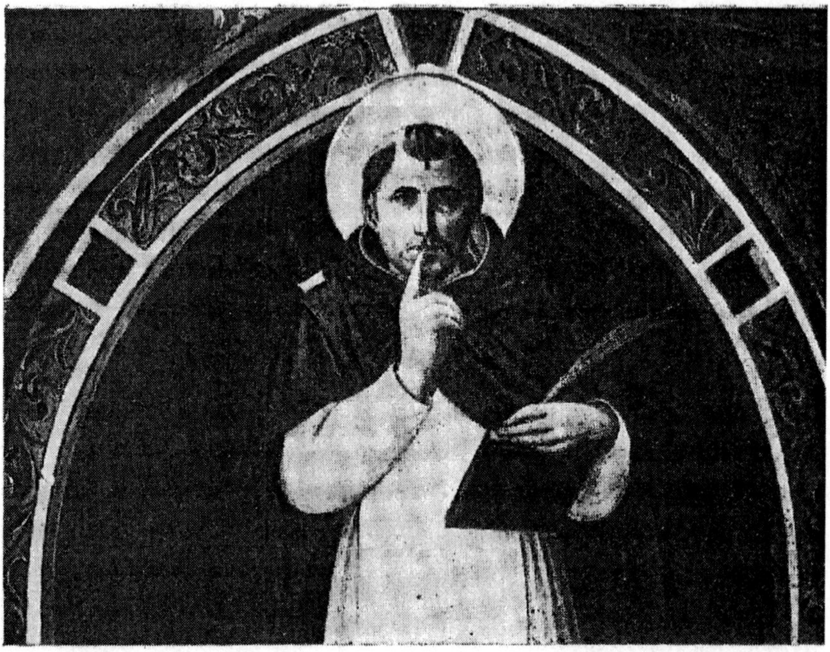

W.L. WILMSHURST

The Ceremony of Initiation

REVISITED BY

ROBERT LOMAS

Dowager

Copyright Main Text © Robert Lomas 2013

Copyright Appendix Text © W.L. Wilmshurst 1932

The right of Robert Lomas to be identified as the Author of the Work has been asserted by him in accordance with the Copyright, Designs and Patents Act 1988.

First published in 2013

by Dowager Books

All rights reserved. No part of this publication may be reproduced, stored in a retrieval system, or transmitted in any form or by any means without the prior written permission of the publisher, nor be otherwise circulated in any form of binding or cover other than that in which it is published and without a similar condition being imposed on the subsequent purchaser.

ISBN-13: 978-1493794591

ISBN-10: 1493794590

Printed by Amazon CreateSpace

DOWAGER BOOKS

www.dowager.com

Dedicated to
Elaine Ann in a Special year.

Acknowledgements

I am grateful to W. Bro Allister Cranna for encouraging me to undertake this book and for his helpful comments on the first draft

I should also like to thank my brethren at the Lodge of Living Stones, who have spent many lodge meetings in discussions about W.L.Wilmshurst and his teachings with me to help us all better understand The Craft, and my trusty editor John Wheelwright for tidying up my work with unfailing good humour.

CONTENTS

PREFACE	1
INTRODUCTION	3
PART I	12
1. Your Admission to the Lodge	12
2. The Prayer of Dedication	13
3. The Mystical Journey	14
4. The Professions of Freedom, Motive and Perseverance	16
5. The Advance from West to East	17
6. Your Obligation	18
7. Your Restoration to Light	21
SUMMARY OF PART I	23
PART II	25
8. The Greater and the Lesser Lights	25
9. The Entrustment with the Secrets	30
10. Your Testing by the Wardens	33
11. Your Investiture with an Apron	35
12. The Charge in the North-East Corner	37
13. The Working Tools	40
14. The Tracing Board	41
CONCLUSION	44

APPENDIX	47
INTRODUCTION	51
PART I	60
1. – The Admission	60
2. – The Prayer of Dedication	61
3. – The Perambulation or Mystical Journeying	62
4. – The Professions of Freedom, Motive, and Perseverance	65
5. – The Advance from West to East	66
6. – The Obligation	67
7. – The Restoration to Light	70
SUMMARY OF PART I	72
PART II	73
8. – The Revelation of the Greater and the Lesser Lights	74
9. – The Entrustment with the Secrets	79
10. – The Testing by the Wardens	82
11. – The Investure with the Apron	84
12. – The Charge in the N.E. Corner	86
13. – The Working Tools	90
14. – The Tracing Board	92
CONCLUSION	95

PREFACE

If you have recently been made a Mason, and if you are anything like me, you will wonder what the First Degree was all about. These notes are a summary of the wisdom of the founding master of the Lodge of Living Stones, Walter Leslie Wilmshurst. They were written to help you, and every newly made Mason, to understand the deeper implications of the Craft. Brethren who have been Masons for some time, and who wish to better understand the purpose and the meaning of the Initiation Ceremony, might also find his ideas helpful.

The Lodge of Living Stones occasionally welcomes new Initiates into the Lodge. With that in mind I decided to revisit the teaching of the Lodge's Founding Master Bro. Walter Leslie Wilmshurst and to present it afresh for our Candidates.

Freemasonry is one of the oldest spiritual self-help systems in the Western world (the earliest documents show it started in Aberdeen in the fifteenth century), and it has refined its methods of teaching to a high level. It uses multi-layered ritual and powerful emotive symbols to help you know yourself and realise your potential. It addresses the spiritual issues which lie at the heart of every religion and also at the centre of modern physics. I have found that both religious metaphors and mathematical equations have helped me to understand the nature of The Great Architect and the human quest for the truth about reality.

Bro. Wilmshurst's aim in compiling this guide to the Masonic system of instruction was to draw aside the veil of allegory and symbolism that, combined with the arcane language used in the ritual, can make the Initiation Ceremony seem confusing when you first meet it. He decided to try to reveal the spirit of the ritual and to uncover its subsurface significance. How successful he was I will leave you to decide. But he was an Edwardian solicitor, spending his whole working life in Huddersfield, so his writing style is a little formal, which is why I decided to express his ideas in a more modern idiom so that you can benefit from his insights. (I have included his original essay in the Appendix on p. 47 below.) He was a strongly committed Christian, so he likes to draw on New Testament metaphor, but he was also widely read in other spiritual traditions and uses them as well.

This essay is a mix of Bro. Walter's ideas and mine. Sometimes, where I differ from his view, I have quoted him directly, but when we agree I have offered my understanding of what he said, in my words.

I hope you will enjoy reliving your peculiar moment and refreshing your memory of the key symbolic points of the Initiation ceremony.

Robert Lomas

INTRODUCTION

The First Degree Ceremony is a ritual used by a Lodge to receive a Candidate both into itself and into Freemasonry universal. It is intended to introduce you to a system of knowledge and self-discipline which aims to clarify your way of thinking and transform your mind from a state of darkness into one of light. If you work at learning to understand and follow the Craft's teachings it can enhance your knowledge of yourself and the universe you live in.

Initiation means to go inwards, to reach beyond the merely material aspects of things, and marks the beginning (*initium*) of a new order of consciousness. It could equally well be called Regeneration or Rebirth, and it has a parallel in the religious sacrament of Baptism. And, just as the baptism of a new Christian is performed at the West end of a Church, so a Masonic Candidate enters the Lodge in the symbolic West. The Masonic ceremony provides an answer to that wish that the Candidate professes to hold dear: the wish to find light and truth. That wish is expressed in an ancient prayer, used in the regions of the East, praying:

From the unreal lead me to the Real;
From the darkness lead me to light;
From the mortal bring me to Immortality!

Past Masters of the Lodge have interviewed you to see if you hold an aspiration to seek light and have judged you motivated enough to be ready for Initiation. To be accepted for Initiation, your attitude must take the form of an intelligent expectation that spiritual good will come to you, and a belief that Freemasonry can satisfy your sacred hunger. You have been judged not to be seeking material or social advantage, nor simply seeking to satisfy idle curiosity about what we do in our guarded and blacked-out Temples. The Lodge believes you are ready to benefit from

Initiation, are genuinely seeking enlightenment and are prepared to work for it.

As a Candidate for Initiation you must realise that whatever academic or scientific learning you possess, whatever philosophical ideas you hold, whatever religious creed you profess before Initiation will not necessarily help you find truth. There is something more for you to learn, and the purpose of the Craft in general (and this Lodge in particular) is to help you to understand what this is. This does not imply that your previous convictions were false; you may well find you knew many concepts that were already true. But if any concepts were mistaken, you will learn how to change them. You must be prepared to discover that some of your most deeply rooted ideas may be only partial understandings of truth. They might be so limited that they obstruct the wider vision you are seeking. If you insist on clinging to them you may block your own view of light and truth. If you are to profit by the light towards which the Craft will try to lead you, you must be prepared to keep your mind open and make the ritual mental self-surrender as your understanding increases. We all tend to feel certain of ourselves, wise in our own conceits, and are unaware that we have much to unlearn – and this limits our ability to be taught. This is why from early times Candidates for Initiation have been called 'children' and encouraged to so regard themselves.

The disrobing of your body before the Ceremony is symbolic of the mental undressing required of you to open yourself to learning. You have to abandon self-will and allow yourself to be taken where you are led and do what you are told to do. This lesson in meekness and docility symbolises how your mind should follow truth wherever it leads, even into perilous places and towards ideas not recognised by the orthodoxies of the world without. True Initiation involves a spiritual adventure, a voyage of the mind into what you have never before experienced. It leads to regions where he who carries the least burdens travels farthest, where he who casts away the most conceit acquires the most benefit. If your heart is hungry it will be filled the good things from which the intellectually rigid are precluded. If you are single-minded you will find wisdom has ways of revealing itself that the conventionally learned do not understand.

The readjustment you need to make will be a gradual process. You will not be called to do sudden violence to your ideas, but to adapt gradually to the new conditions and be transformed by a slow renewal of your mind. This is symbolically demonstrated as you progress from Degree to Degree. In the First Degree, only certain parts of your body are bared; in the Second, other and complementary parts will be opened to knowledge. Not until the Third Degree is maximum openness required, and by that time you will have learnt the nature of self-surrender and be properly prepared to face the larger sacrifice that the sublime Third Degree involves.

But what of the Ceremony? In the early days of Freemasonry there were no formally printed ritual books. The working was passed on orally. The form of words employed was (and is) the least important part of the ceremony. More important is the ability of the Initiator, and the supporting officers of the Lodge, to infuse spiritual fervour and emotional momentum into what is done, so that the ritual penetrates your heart, stimulates your mind and awakens basic truths in your soul. For this to happen you must be a fit and proper person . . . and properly prepared for the revelation.

In the Irish, the Scottish and many Continental Masonic Constitutions no set ritual is used. Basic landmarks and age-old usages are observed, but for the rest (e.g. the various charges, explanations, and entrustings) the wording of the ceremony is left to the inspiration and emotion of the moment.

English traditional ritual, with slight local variations, embodies all these landmarks and usages, and has been compiled with inspired skill and wisdom. Do not treat it superficially, or think of it as a memory task to be reeled off non-stop; that would be to miss the purpose and beauty of its import. The ritual of the Lodge of Living Stones is built up from fourteen distinct 'movements' or episodes, in two series of seven. I will now explain them according to the ideas of Bro. Wilmshurst.

The first series is associated with relieving your state of darkness. The emotion of the working follows an ascending emotional wave that climaxes at the moment of your symbolic restoration to light.

The second series is concerned with more practical matters of instruction. It is a descending sequence, allowing your emotional billow to gradually die away and leave you filled with new perceptions.

Do not be surprised if it takes you some time to understand it, or if you have to visit and see others undergoing the same ceremony, and if you need time to reflect on your understanding, before you do understand it.

The sequence of these episodes is as follows (notice what a large range of ideas has been compressed into a short ceremony):

YOUR STATE OF DARKNESS
1. Your Admission to the Lodge.
2. The Prayer of Dedication.
3. The Mystical Journey (or Perambulation).
4. The Professions of Freedom, Motive and Perseverance.
5. The Advance from West to East.
6. Your Obligation.
7. Your Restoration to Light.

YOUR STATE OF LIGHT
8. The Greater and the Lesser Lights.
9. The Entrustment with the Secrets.
10. Your Testing by the Wardens.
11. Your Investiture with an Apron.
12. The Charge in the North-East Corner.
13. The Working Tools.
14. The Tracing Board.

Each of the fourteen incidents provides material for extensive reflection and commentary, but, in these notes I will make only brief comments on each one.

The separation of the Ceremony into two main sections, the 'state of darkness' and the 'state of light', symbolises a cosmic truth about human life whilst maintaining a historical correspondence with the Ancient Mysteries.

Cosmically, all human life begins its quest for light and truth in a state of darkness about its nature, its purpose and its destiny. We are born blind or hoodwinked about our *raison d'être*. The Ancients taught that we have all drunk the water of forgetfulness before being born in our flesh. Our lack of knowledge of our purpose, our hoodwinked fumbling, our searching for we know not what, continues until the disillusionments of existence awake us to the fact that there may be something higher worth hunting for. This preliminary condition of mind and soul the Initiates likened to being in a place which they called 'the Hall of Ignorance' or 'the Hall of Truth in Darkness'. There we grope for the light and wisdom that are around us, but which we cannot discover because our faculties are not trained to perceive them.

Later on, when we turn to the quest for better things, we are taught the science of them, and are said to have entered the 'Hall of Learning' or the 'Hall of Truth in Light'. By this time we are no longer ignorantly groping in the dark, but have become driven by an enlightened resolve to find the reality which casts the flickering shadows on the wall of our Platonic cave.

These two conditions, the first of groping ignorantly with blinded eyes for the reality behind temporal existence, and the second of seeking it intelligently with the opened eyes of the Initiate, are reproduced in the two divisions of the First Degree Ceremony. But there is also a third condition – which for you, as a novice, is a long way off – that is beyond the scope of this present guidance. Enough to say that its attainment is described as entering the 'Hall of Wisdom', and it is possible for Master Masons who have passed through the two previous 'Halls', and whose search is rewarded by discovering ultimate secret of life.

Before the ceremony began there was a preliminary routine, called the preparation of the Candidate, which is a necessary part of the ritual. I will explain this before looking at the fourteen stages of the ceremony itself.

The Craft requires every Candidate for Initiation to come 'properly prepared'. Every ancient and modern Initiation system insists on intensive preparation. For those who desire light, a preliminary orientation of will, heart and mind is indispensable to fulfilling their desire. 'Prepare ye the way of the Lord!' is the Biblical confirmation of what the Ancient Mysteries required and what the Craft inculcates. When the Master of the Lodge dispatches his Deacon to prepare the Candidate for his reception, he is echoing and giving a personal value to words of impersonal and cosmic application.

The ritual brings together various streams of influence, the chief of which is the traditional method, often known as the 'Secret Doctrine'. Common to all Ancient Mysteries and Initiation systems from the dawn of history, this method holds some knowledge in reserve from the masses of the people; it constitutes stronger 'meat' and imparts deeper truths than the simple instruction, or 'milk', provided for popular use. Students of the history of religion know that behind the exoteric doctrine of every great spiritual Teacher there has always been an esoteric counterpart for advanced disciples, and elements of this ancient esoteric wisdom can be found in Hermeticism, the Hebrew Cabala, Rosicrucianism and survivals from mediaeval Guild Masonry. The Holy Scriptures of Judaism and Christianity contain such teaching and have served to nourish the religious life of the West as a unifying and explanatory 'great light'.

Our Masonic Ritual, as the offspring of these sources, uses the language of its parents, speaking in the terms or symbols of one or another of them. All these sources have been stewards of the same Mysteries, and they proclaim the same Truth. Hence the lack of concern by the Craft with the particular beliefs of the Candidate. There is only one truth to be found, but there are many spiritual paths towards it. Freemasons respect all religions and hope to share what they find in common, rather than quarrel over what they think might be different.

The mental preparation of you, as a Candidate, started long before the Ceremony began. Your Masonic sponsors tested and vouched for your readiness for Initiation. They will have given you a broad idea of what is involved, and will have assured themselves that you will respond sympathetically to what will be done.

In the Lodge of Living Stones we pay close attention to your symbolic preparation. So you were taken to a quiet ante-room and left alone for some time to compose your mind, read some sentences warning you of the solemnity of what was about to happen and reminding you of the need to proceed in a spirit of meekness and confidence. You were given an opportunity to withdraw if you were in any way uncomfortable.

You will have been interviewed by a Deacon and asked for your decision. As you desired to proceed, you were then asked to write brief replies to some such questions as:

> What is your view of the purpose of human life and the nature of human destiny?
> What is your object in seeking to be initiated?
> What may the Craft hope to receive from you in return for what you expect to receive from it?

The Deacon will have asked you to surrender all your metals and money. After that, the formal preparation of your person proceeded with solemnity. The reason for each separate act of preparation was briefly explained by the Deacon.

The tradition that has grown up in the Lodge of Living Stones since Wilmshurst's time attaches great importance to the performance of the Deacon's ministrations in creating a favourable mental condition for you before you enter the Lodge. Hence, the Junior Deacon who prepared you is normally stationed in the West of the Lodge, where the 'Master appointed him to serve at the right hand of his chief Warden and to be that Warden's messenger'. He carries the Master's commands from the West to the South, so that the will, the wisdom, and the love of the Master is transmitted throughout the Temple, and the whole Lodge is vivified.

When acting as an officer of the Lodge the deacon is a ray sent forth from the throne of Wisdom, carrying messages from the Centre of Being to the outward mind of the brethren. He goes forth as a thought-flash from the Mind of the Great Architect in its providential care for the soul of each Brother, reaching into your mind through your human emotion. He is sent forth as a messenger of The Great Architect to prepare His way. For the meaning of the title Deacon is 'Dia-konos': one who comes beating through 'even as the vibrations of the Divine Mind beat through into the heart of man to bid it turn Eastwards'.

The Master has entrusted him with a white rod as an emblem of peace. When ordered by the Master, he goes out of the Temple to bring the covenant of peace to you whose heart is moved to turn from darkness to light. It is his duty to prepare the way for you and make it straight, so that he may help you to find that which your heart seeks.

> He divested you of everything with no place in the Sanctuary, and robed you in the raiment of the poor in spirit.
>
> With mercy he shielded your eyes from that light which was as yet too bright for you to bear.
>
> He loosened the shoes from your feet that you might learn to walk on holy ground.
>
> He led you to the threshold of the Mysteries and presented you properly prepared and coming in the name of light, so you could approach without peril to your soul.
>
> He supported and encouraged you on the path to the East, teaching you the first steps to the Master, and did not leave you until you had received sight.

Before you entered the Lodge the atmosphere of the Temple was prepared, to ensure it was peaceful and free of commotion. While the Deacon was helping you ready yourself outside the Lodge, the Worshipful Master called for silence and asked the brethren assembled to reflect upon the nature of the work in hand and unite with you, so that the work would be spiritually effective.

Even though many of the brethren did not take an officer's role in your initiation, together they were active participants in the mystery of your Initiation. The power of their united and concentrated thoughts will have impressed on you new, spiritual perceptions. The whole Lodge, officers, brethren and visitors focused their silent mental co-operation on working the mystery of Initiation for you.

I will now explain how your ceremony was structured.

PART I

1. Your Admission to the Lodge

Once you were prepared and blindfolded you were led to the door of the Lodge. It was locked and guarded. The door was firmly closed in your face, so you were forced to 'meet with opposition' (as the Entered Apprentice Lecture says) and could not simply enter.

When you turned from the world without to the world within your first discovery was that your way was blocked. What blocked it? What does the door of the Lodge symbolise?

It symbolises obstructive elements in yourself. You were made to recognise that any opposition to your spiritual advancement comes from within yourself and can only be overcome by your own efforts. (This is why you were required to give the knocks yourself – they should never be given for you by anyone else.)

The purpose of this episode is said, in the Entered Apprentice Lecture, to be subjective and mystical. The knocks are to be interpreted in the light of the Scriptural direction, 'Ask and ye shall have; Seek and ye shall find; Knock and it shall be opened to you'. This threefold instruction corresponds to the triple knocks, and to your own triple faculties as a Candidate. You 'ask' with the prayerful aspirations of your heart. You 'seek' with the intellectual activities of your mind. And you 'knock' with the force of your bodily energies. If you hope to find the light within you, you must devote your entire being to the quest.

This symbolic opposition at the door of the Lodge is true to life and psychology. We all erect mental barriers. The habitual thought-methods, prejudices, preconceptions and fixed ideas which we indulge in the course of life in the outer world become obstructions to the perception of the world within. They create mental deposits that harden and obscure the clearer vision that you might possess, but for your self-created limitations. We erect and tyle our own door against ourselves. we block our own light, and eventually find ourselves confronted by darkness and opposition that we ourselves have created. When we seek light and truth these barriers have to be broken down by our own efforts and the force of our own persistent 'knocks'.

The knocks may be thought of as vibrations. Persistent vibrations, in a given direction will eventually break down whatever is opposed to them, whether physical or mental. Vibrations of faith remove mountains. Vibrations of intellectual energy result in solutions to problems. Vibrations of emotion break into the hearts of others. Vibrations of spiritual aspiration penetrate into higher worlds and open the doors to them. All this is signified by the simple action of you, the Candidate, meeting with opposition at the door of the Lodge and gaining admission as the result of your own symbolic knocks.

2. The Prayer of Dedication

After you entered the Lodge the first act of the ceremony was a prayer by the assembled Brethren. It dealt with strength, wisdom and beauty asking:

> That you, the Candidate (already elected to formal membership of the Craft) would be given the strength to become spiritually incorporated into the Great Brotherhood; and
>
> That you would be endowed with an influx of wisdom to enable you to manifest the beauty of truth.

This prayer had implications, despite its brevity and simplicity: it contained the first reference to a trinity of Wisdom, Strength and Beauty that you will hear more of later, and it prayed that you might become a living manifestation of that trio of virtues.

Moreover, there is no reference in this prayer to morality or ethical virtues. It invokes something loftier than those: the gift of the Spirit. It sets the tone of both the Ceremony and your Masonic life.

You should notice that it is not a prayer offered *by* you. You are only asked to 'kneel and listen' to it. It is a prayer *for* you, and for the Craft itself. It is a prayer that the spiritual efficiency of the whole Fraternity may be strengthened by your joining it. Every Brother present united with the Chaplain to create what our Founding Master called 'a strong tension of aspiration' that the prayer would be answered in the joint interest of the Craft and its new member. Later on, you were encouraged to make the prayer your own, remembering that it was once offered over you on behalf of the whole Craft whilst you still dwelt in darkness and helplessness. Now you are part of that Craft, it is your duty to justify the invocation that was so solemnly made on your behalf.

3. The Mystical Journey

Once the prayer was offered you were asked where, at any time of danger and difficulty, you put your trust. This must have made you wonder what was about to happen to you. The question was to test if you were prepared to face the trials of Initiation, and you were encouraged to confirm that you had faith that there was a source of order in the universe that you could trust. The answer had to be your own, and the implication of the question was that, had you been unable to answer it sincerely, then you would have been refused entry to the Lodge. The reason is simple: if you do not believe that there is a purpose to the universe, then how can you hope to learn anything about something that you do not believe exists? You obviously did hold such a belief, as your answer was satisfactory.

Once that issue was dealt with, you were taken on a journey. This is known to Masons as the Perambulation.

What dangers and difficulties were you about to be exposed to? In our Ceremony they were theoretical and symbolic. But Bro. Wilmshurst informs us that the Initiation Rites of the Ancient Mysteries (of which ours are a faint echo) were exacting, realistic and frightening. They tested mental stability and moral fitness, and they made sure that Candidates for Initiation into the secrets and mysteries of their own being had a stable faith and moral centre – in other words a sound mind in a sound body. This was to avoid unfit persons being rashly subjected to experiences for which they were unsuited.

This is why you had to make a public declaration of faith and were passed in review before the Lodge as the Ceremony began, so that the Lodge could be satisfied of your mental and physical fitness. But there is also another reason for the ceremonial perambulation. The journey you took round the Lodge was a symbolic representation of your life-journeyings in the outer world before you requested Initiation into the inner world.

You should notice two things about your symbolic journey. First, even though you were in a state of darkness you were not alone; you had with you an enlightened guide. And you were watched over by a host of witnesses, all keenly anxious for your spiritual advancement and eventual restoration to light. The significance of this is that you have within you an invisible guide, and your soul's upward struggles are observed by many unseen well-wishers.

Secondly, in the course of your symbolic journey you were led to each Warden in turn. Then you roused him from silence and encouraged him to speak to you. You did this by repeating the knocks you had given at the door of the Lodge. But those knocks had been addressed to an inert door, now you applied them to a living being: the Warden. This reminds you that your efforts to turn away from the outer world and discover the light of the inner one require you not only to overcome your self-created opposition but also to awaken the dormant energies within yourself.

You will learn more about those latent energies. For the moment, though, it is enough for you to recognise that your desire for light awakens within you slumbering potencies that in the future will be stimulated to promote your spiritual advancement. In other writings Bro. Wilmshurst points out that in you reside two dormant principles, represented by the two Wardens, which it is possible to provoke into activity to speed you on your way with the mystical greeting: 'Pass, Good Report!'

The expression 'Good Report' which was used to describe you is a modern version of an ancient mystical form. It means more than 'good reputation'. it implies that the your nature is animated by spiritual sincerity, rings true like a bell, and sounds forth a convincing note when it speaks. That is why you were called upon to speak so that the Warden could decide if you were 'true of voice' and qualified to be passed on.

'Say something that I may see you,' said Socrates to a shy youth who sought his instruction, for your speech describes you to the sensitive ear that can judge the speaker's sincerity and spiritual status. This was why you were required to speak out to the Wardens.

4. The Professions of Freedom, Motive and Perseverance

After both Wardens had satisfied themselves of your fitness for advancement to the East, you were presented to the Master for Initiation. But before the Master accepted you, you had to pledge yourself to three requirements:

- That you sought the light voluntarily, for its own sake, and from no unworthy motive;
- That you sought it for two reasons: to gain knowledge of yourself, and ritually to make yourself of more extensive service to humanity;

That you would persevere along the path about to be disclosed to you (which means persevering not just through the formal Ceremony, but throughout your subsequent daily life).

You had to answer these questions spontaneously and without prompting. They involved far-reaching personal commitments, so it was important that you did not answer lightly and were not under duress.

The second promise was important in that you agreed that any higher knowledge you acquired would be used in the service of humanity. But you can only serve humanity when you know how to. This service does not mean public activity to try and convince others of your worth; it means service undertaken without fuss or self-aggrandisement. You need knowledge of yourself in order to serve others effectively. That knowledge is not given you for selfish purposes but for use in the selfless service of humanity. The enlightenment of Initiation is not for personal benefit; it is a trust for the general good. Every Initiate becomes salt and seasoning in a corruptible world. You are called upon not to hide your light but to let it shine before mankind so that they may see in you as an example worth following.

Service to others is the ulterior motive of the Mysteries, but that service can take many forms and can be rendered in higher ways than the ordinary altruistic activity of public charity. Of these you will learn more later. But never forget this: at the threshold of your Masonic life, you pledged to become a servant of humanity.

5. The Advance from West to East

This advance is a small episode in the ceremony, and one which you may not have noticed at the time. But it has far-reaching symbolic significance as the climax of the mystical path you had been blindly following. You travelled around the Lodge three times, before your hand was finally taken by the Senior Warden, who presented you to the Master for a mark of favour.

THE CEREMONY OF INITIATION

The journeying around the Lodge symbolised your life wanderings since you were born into this world (in the 'West' of the Lodge). It demonstrated that you had passed blindly, though with unseen guidance, through regions of darkness (the 'North'), as well as through regions of less or greater enlightenment (the 'South', 'West' and 'East'). Because you were in state of personal darkness you remained ignorant of where you were going or what the purpose of your life was. You never knew at any given moment if you were near or far from your life's true goal. This symbolic journeying represents a human life without purpose. Until your eyes are opened to the plan of it, you do not know whether any event in your personal life experience is drawing you nearer to or farther from the goal you are unwittingly seeking.

Your ignorant perambulations, your circular wanderings without forward progress, buffeted by fortune and exposed to tests of character, finally terminate in the decision to move from the darkness of the West to the light of the East. Your steps, though irregular, were towards the light in the East. Intellectually and emotionally you were still wobbling from side to side before you were shown how to achieve a stable foothold and find the straight way. But, because you were bent on finding the way to the light of the East at all costs, you will assuredly get there. And you will arrive in the East bearing a certificate of fitness for higher things conferred by the Senior Warden, who presented you to the Worshipful Master as a fit and proper person and properly prepared to be made a Mason.

So you arrive at the Altar in the Centre of the Lodge.

6. Your Obligation

Bro. Wilmshurst reminds us that it has always been the practice of mystery traditions and secret Orders, to demand a vow of silence and secrecy from its Candidates before the conferment of Initiation and the sharing of secret information. So it is with Freemasonry.

The Obligation you took might be thought of as perpetuating the usual covenant of secrecy required by new members of the old Trade Guilds to guard the privileges of that Guild and protect technical trade secrets. Our speculative Craft follows the Operatives in this respect, but the reason for being solemnly obligated runs much deeper than a need for silence about the formal secrets of the Order.

The main purpose was to impress in you, a newcomer to the path of light and self-knowledge, a sense of the value of silence about the new perceptions that will come to you. You will encounter new ideas and experience mental reactions as a result of them. This silence and secrecy are imposed not in the interest of the Fraternity at large (which can suffer little from your indiscretions) but in your own interest. Experience will teach you the deep value of silent reflection. Light and Wisdom are not acquired from anything that can be shown or told to you. They come from the gradual impact of new ideas and their gradual assimilation into your mind, and to help this your mental energies should be conserved, not frittered away in talk.

In the world outside the Lodge much energy is wasted in needless private chatter and public utterance, when it might be redirected to higher ends. The way of the inner life, which you symbolically accepted when entering the door of the Lodge, is different. As a Mason you will be called to practice silence and economy of speech and to take moral responsibility for each word you speak. You will be taught to conserve your verbal energy, avoid vapid, frothy exuberance and enter the deep, still waters of knowledge. Silent reflection generates the power needed for speaking with authority and effect when it is needed.

Both the Christian and Jewish Volumes of the Sacred Law declare 'There is a time to be silent and a time to speak', (Ecclesiastes III: 7). The time for silence comes first, for it is not possible to 'speak' at all until, by the discipline of silence, you have acquired the wisdom to know what to say, how, when and to whom to say it, and possess the spiritual momentum to transform ordinary speech into 'words of power'. It is only after you have learned the discipline of silence that 'out of the fullness of the heart the mouth speaketh'.

You, as a newly made brother, in the first flush of your new Masonic life will find new perceptions and ideas welling up in your mind after your Initiation. This will lead you into new areas of thought and fresh fields of study. You might feel a need to share with others things they are just beginning to learn themselves. It is always satisfactory when the forces of Initiation prove effective and kindle your inner fire, but, to curb crude enthusiasm, the Obligation ordains silence until you have sufficient understanding to speak out. That is why the Craft observes a traditional practice of restricting the giving of instruction in Masonic science to Master Masons. When you are awarded Mastership your 'time to speak' will come.

There is a risk attached to premature and unwise speech, and it is highlighted in the penalty of the Obligation. The spiritual intention behind the penalty implies that, if you are unfaithful to your duty of silence, you could lose the power to use words effectively and instead spread confusion and bewilderment – in modern parlance we might say, learn to engage your brain before opening your mouth By frittering away energy that should be conserved, you can leave yourself spiritually speechless.

Wilmshurst quotes a wise old counsel saying:

> *Word is thrall but Thought makes free;*
> *Hold thy speech, I counsel thee.*

You took your Obligation upon a book that is your symbolic emblem of the Divine Word of your individual faith. By your formal acknowledgement of the authority regulating your oath, you identified yourself with its importance to you. By emulating its purpose, you may eventually recover that Lost Word that Masonry seeks to find, and perhaps in due course be able sound it from your own mouth.

You are sure to remember the difficult posture you were placed in take the Obligation. To help you understand the symbolism of the stance, compare it with the symbolic disrobing you underwent before you entered the Lodge. The changing and progressive nature of both the postures and the degree of disrobing adopted during the three Degrees are deeply significant. They teach that, before you can develop a new regenerate self, your old self-hood must be broken down, its pride humbled, its attachment to external possessions and ingrained mental prejudice cast aside. This is a gradual process. You are never called upon to do anything beyond your immediate powers, but encouraged to follow the principle of 'precept upon precept; line upon line; here a little and there a little'.

The posture (and disrobing) change in each Degree and affect different limbs and parts of your person. In the First Degree only one knee rests on the ground. In the Second it will be the other knee that will mark your progressive humility. In the Third your posture will signify that your humility is total. All resistance of mind and stubbornness of will sink to complete self-surrender to the Sacred Law upon whose symbolic volume you placed first one hand and finally both.

7. Your Restoration to Light

After completing your Obligation you were reminded that for a considerable time you had been in a state of darkness. The whole ceremony is allegory, so don't be so literal-minded as to think this refers just to the few minutes when your sight was hoodwinked for symbolic reasons. The ritual reveals to you a parable of your soul's development, pointing out that that your soul has hitherto lived in a state of darkness, and that you will continue in darkness until it regains its spiritual consciousness. This awareness the Craft calls 'light'.

'Our birth is but a sleep and a forgetting', says Wordsworth in *Intimations of Immortality*. Bro. Wilmshurst suggests he might have added that our Initiation is an awakening and a remembering, but it only comes when a latent central 'light' is kindled within us. Then we seek the purpose of our existence, seeking which is the predominant wish of every human heart. While we are in darkness the wish remains dormant until Initiation, when it becomes a conscious urge for knowledge.

That definite urge within your soul became overpowering, so you had no peace until you found what you sought. It drove you to seek Initiation, so that the door opened to your knock and you heard the Master say, 'Let there be light'.

Throughout the ritual 'light' is used to symbolise 'consciousness'. So the words 'Let there be light' symbolise an expansion of consciousness in your mind. And consciousness is present to some extent in everything, from microbe to man, but mankind is evolving a consciousness that is capable of advancing further – beyond the human.

Our First Degree introduces you to this expansion beyond your normal mentality. The Second Degree takes you further. The Third facilitates a 'raising' to higher consciousness still. But the Supreme Degree of the Royal Arch reaches a final sublime 'exaltation' of consciousness for which the prior Craft Degrees prepare you.

The sequence of grades develops a progressive advance from your normal mentality to the heights of spiritual consciousness, an advance which is biblically called 'ascending the Hill of the Lord'. Each of our Masonic ceremonies is designed to promote a regular step on that ascent.

How far your climb will be promoted by a particular ceremony, how far your conscience will be quickened and expanded, depends upon three conditions.

1. The help of The Great Architect;
2. The readiness of your mind;
3. The efficiency of the Lodge and the Initiating Master in bringing these two into union.

The development of your spiritual consciousness may not come about during the ceremony. Often it emerges slowly from the darkness of your clouded understanding. In the words of Masonic ritual, the Sun at the centre of your personal system mounts to the meridian gradually: first there is a dawn, then a gradual rising and a scattering of the darkness before the full light of high twelve.

The applause at the removal of the hoodwink is called 'firing'. All the brethren present take part in the symbolic 'giving of fire' to you at that moment of restoration to light. It is a discharge of the tension which the assembly built up during the ceremony, an outward expression of their co-operation with the Initiating Master in bringing you from darkness to light. You may think of it as the sound of your inward fetters breaking, uplifting your soul to enable you to say 'Whereas before I was blind, now I see!'

Summary of Part I

Your restoration to light is the peak-point of the Ceremony and concludes its first portion. Symbolically you have taken seven ascending steps up the mystical mountain during your symbolic 'state of darkness'.

These were:
1. Your Admission to the Lodge;
2. The Prayer of Dedication;
3. The Mystical Journey (or Perambulation);
4. The Professions of Freedom, Motive, and Perseverance;
5. The Advance from West to East;
6. Your Obligation;
7. Your Restoration to Light.

This working dramatised in symbolic, ritual form the path you must follow under the stress of your deepest heart-impulses to turn your discontent with the outside world into a quest to discover the world within yourself. It explains your nature and past life, indicates how you can bring about a re-orientation, and gives you hope that you will succeed. You learned that that you have to empty yourself of your old self so as to divest and detach yourself from your past acquisitions, whether intellectual or material. Your 'personal comforts' are restored to you later on, but they take on new values for you. Like Job in the Old Testament, you have been stripped of your worldly assets to serve a higher good. This is a great adventure of faith: you will have to let go of what you have, trust yourself to invisible guidance and remain resolute to find what you seek and break down opposition between you and your goal. By dedicating yourself to light and becoming a light-bearer, you will become an instrument of human service at a higher level than you could ever render before Initiation.

This is the path of true Initiation taught by this Ceremony. It involves blinding your eyes, baring your heart, and tyling your mind to things external, so they can all be opened to things internal in a true Restoration to light. As Bro. Wilmshurst puts it.

> *Then comes the Sun's light to our hut*
> *When fast the senses' door is shut.*
> *For such a pure and perfect guest*
> *The emptiest room is furnished best.*

The spiritual quest acted out in the ceremony makes it more than a formality. It offers a goal worth pursuing when it is performed with understanding and its lessons are transplanted into your daily conduct. If you are not changed by it, you profane it; you increase your own darkness and are no different from the unenlightened. But if it causes that Sun which glows at your centre to rise in your consciousness, then it puts into your hands a means of grace of great value.

PART II

The remainder of the Ceremony is a series of seven descending steps that consolidate your newly won 'state of light' and instruct you how to conserve, nourish and develop what you have just glimpsed.

8. The Greater and the Lesser Lights

Until you experience the actual 'restoration to light' you will not comprehend it. It is inexpressible. It must be experienced before the psychological state it induces in you can be understood. Even then you will struggle to describe it.

Perhaps an analogy may help you understand the enlargement of consciousness which Initiation causes. It is a rebirth of your spiritual nature and is akin to physical birth; Wilmshurst describes it as '"birth" repeated upon a higher level of the spiral of creation'. When you were physically born you were initiated into a new state of consciousness which you had not previously experienced. Try to remember what it felt like before you were born . . . you cannot remember. It took many years before your consciousness developed in its new environment, and your eyes began to focus upon things around you. Immediately after birth you were only vaguely conscious, and most of your memories of this time will be incoherent fragments. It took time and practice for your brain to accustom itself and its eyesight to its surroundings and for your memory and understanding to develop. Your psychological rebirth is similar.

Individual experience varies, but broadly you pass into a state of awareness that something of an expanding and illuminating nature has happened to you. Often you cannot tell what it is, let alone explain it to others. You felt an upheaval from within, a shifting of your focus of consciousness to a different level. You feel a sense of liberation from your mental limitations which carries a promise of wider mental vision and deeper understanding. But, above all, you feel inexplicable happiness. This is a crude description of what a properly prepared Candidate might experience as the outcome of his Initiation. In biblical language, you were one of those who dwelt in darkness but have now seen a great light. You cannot yet say what that light is or explain your perception in detail. You only know you have received your sight and, whereas you were relatively blind, now you are beginning to see.

Few Candidates experience the 'restoration to light' to this extent during the ceremony. However, subsequent reflection on your new experience will steady your emotions and help your mental sight to adjust until you begin to perceive new truths. Like a baby, you must learn to adjust to the objects around you.

As your mental vision clears, great primary truths gradually emerge. These truths were introduced to you during the second part of the Ceremony. Symbolically they are called the 'Three Great Emblematic Lights'. These symbols were revealed by the Master and were the first objects you saw after being restored to light. You were in a kneeling position, and facing the East. The great lights were pointed out and briefly explained whilst you were still kneeling. The symbolic reason for this, is that it is appropriate to contemplate fundamental truths in an attitude of humility, when mentally you are on your knees. The Three Great Lights are the first objects presented to your newly restored perception while you are kneeling towards the East.

These Three Great Lights are your Volume of the Sacred Law, the Square and the Compasses. They are displayed as organically combined: your chosen Volume of the Sacred Law lay on the altar to form a base for the other two great lights. The Compasses were partially concealed by the Square.

Bro. Wilmshurst interprets these three symbolic emblems thus:
(1) The Volume of the Sacred Law (VSL) embodies the Divine Law, as revealed to your chosen tradition, but has universal significance. For Masons it is a visible emblem of an invisible Cosmic Law through which order is manifest in the Universe. It symbolises the Great Architect, whose Law underlies everything and is the basis of being. 'Law' can take many forms, and you should not limit your ideas to any one of them, but think of the VSL as symbolising them all. This includes physical law, intellectual law, moral law, and the dual qualities of Justice and Mercy, Severity and Love, which characterise the nature of The Great Architect.

The Craft's conception of the 'Sacred Law' is broad. Masonry does not treat the Bible as the only expression of it. The Holy Scriptures of any religion are exposed in the Lodge in place of or alongside the Bible, according the wishes of the brethren. The principle is that you may be obligated upon the particular revelation of Cosmic Law which you recognise as true for yourself. This makes it binding on your conscience. Alternative sets of Scriptures are kept, so that a Jew may be obligated upon the Pentateuch, a Moslem upon the Koran, an Indian upon the Vedas or Puranas, and so on. The Volume of the Sacred Law is a symbol of the existence of a Supreme Order or Cosmic Purpose within the Universe.

(2) The Compasses resting upon the Volume of the Sacred Law represent the Divine Spirit issuing forth from the Great Architect to manifest, both cosmically and in the individual, whilst functioning in accordance with the Divine Law.

(3) The Square, set opposite to the Compasses but inextricably conjoined with them, represents cosmic Matter, by which means the Divine Spirit takes material form.

Together the Three Great Lights reveal a Cosmic Purpose: i.e., Spirit and Matter working together according to Divine Law to realise the intention of the Divine Plan.

What is that Divine Plan? It is the construction of a perfect Universe, occupied by perfect beings. It is a Universe in which animating spirit and material form stand in perfect balance. Both are aspects of a Divine Order, are a perfect expression of the Divine Thought and a fitting tabernacle for the Great Architect to dwell in.

Masonically, we speak of the Universe as an unfinished Cosmic Temple being built in accordance with the Divine Law using the Divine Compasses and Square. This basic tenet of Masonic philosophy is the first 'secret' revealed to you. It is displayed in the symbolic guise of the Triune of Great Lights. As a Mason, it is now your duty to co-operate with the Great Architect in executing the Divine plan and completing the Great Cosmic Temple.

Once you had been shown the Three Great Lights (or, as you now understand them, the three great Cosmic Principles) you were placed to the North of the Master's chair, facing South, and shown Three Lesser Lights burning in different parts of the Lodge. These Lesser Lights stand in correspondence with the three great ones. They are the Sun, represented by the Junior Warden in the South, the Moon represented by the Senior Warden in the West, and the Master of the Lodge in the East. The Sun to rule the day, the Moon to rule the night and the Master to rule his Lodge and instruct his brethren in Freemasonry. They are to remind you of three great Cosmic Principles that are present within you. The Universe is the Macrocosm (or the great image of the Divine Intent); you are the Microcosm (the image in miniature of the same Intent). In you reside three ritual 'lights', (the Square, the Compasses and the Volume of the Sacred Law), and they work together to enable you to take part in The Great Architect's plan. You have been entrusted with the Compasses of a discerning Mind to direct your personal life and a Square of bodily form on which you can work to create a living stone to fit into the structure of the Cosmic Temple, and you have a chosen a Volume of the Sacred Law to act as a Master Light of Conscience to inform your path of duty.

Three Lesser Lights, or three 'ritual' officers (the Master in the Sacred East, The Senior Warden in the Dark Secular West, and the Junior Warden in the Light of the Noonday Sun), will enable you – as the Lecture of the Degree explains – to perceive the form of the Lodge, to realise the arrangement of its furniture and jewels and to contemplate its length, breadth and height. You will notice that the Brethren are arranged around its sides, and its middle portion is empty, to be illumined by the 'Glory in the Centre'.

This symbolism helps you realise that all the perceived reality of the Cosmos is but an image of yourself, seen from within yourself rather than from the outside. For, just as you are now within the Lodge and able to see what was previously closed to you, so with the help of your inner lights you will be able to know yourself and contemplate the spaciousness of your soul. The ritual and symbols will help you to decide which jewels of character should adorn the inner space of your character, and to understand that your personal faculties are arrayed around your circumference while at your centre blazes a bright Star.

To sum up: the teaching of the Great Lights reveals the basic Laws and Principles of being. The lesser ones are your first lesson in the 'knowledge of yourself'. They teach you that those principles exist within your soul and provide you with lights to shape it into perfection and bring you into harmony with the Cosmic Law.

The concealment of the lower points of the Compasses beneath the Square teaches another important lesson. It implies that the power of your spirit (represented by the Compasses) is as yet prevented from full function by the repressive tendencies of your material body (represented by the Square). In due course this position must be reversed if you are to become a living stone fit to be an integral part of the Cosmic Temple. As you awake to the possibilities of your spiritual principle it must be freed from the whims of your flesh. This, you are taught as a Mason, can only be achieved by your own efforts. As you subdue your lower nature, so you will liberate the powers and faculties of your spirit and allow it to rise to mastery over the material forces of your character.

In subsequent Degrees this triumph of the spirit over the body is symbolically 'illuminated' by the points of the Compasses being progressively raised above the Square, first one and then the other, until you are 'able to work with both those points and render the circle of your Masonic conduct complete'.

9. The Entrustment with the Secrets

Having been shown the Greater and Lesser Lights you were warned that you had unknowingly faced serious dangers that you had already overcome. You were shown the poniard that the inner guard used to prick your naked left breast and the cabletow which hung around your neck. These are visible symbols of the spiritual perils you would have faced: swift death by stabbing with the dagger if you rashly rushed towards spiritual experience before you were ready for it and or slow strangulation by the cabletow if you tried to flee from the path of light once you realised it existed. The message is that if you are patient and willing to learn you will receive instruction. Until you gain greater knowledge of yourself and the Cosmic plan you may not realise these perils exist – but they do, and you are advised to accept the warning as a wise counsel from those more advanced than yourself.

When you see the poniard Bro. Wilmshurst suggests you think of the frequent Scriptural references to the two-edged 'sword of the Spirit', and its penetrating power which was said to guard the way to the central 'Tree of Life'. This will help you understand the symbolic use of the poniard in the Ceremony, and why you were made to feel its sharp point when you first entered the Lodge.

The cabletow has considerable symbolic significance. It is so important that it appears in various guises in each of the three degrees, and also in the Royal Arch. Its deeper meaning will become clear when you gain more experience and are judged properly prepared for a suitable teacher to share their knowledge. Biblically, the cabletow is referred to in Ecclesiastes XII: 6 ('Or ever the silver cord is loosed . . .'), and when you understand that text you realise why the 'cord' is used in the ceremonies.

Once you had been alerted to the dangers you had already avoided, the next step was to entrust you with the formal 'secrets' of the Degree. These consist of peculiar marks or signs, that distinguish all Apprentices. In this, and in subsequent Degrees, they are expressed by step, sign, and word. They are not the real secrets, but figurative emblems of them. They symbolise the real secrets, and it is left to you to meditate and deduce those from the insights of your daily personal meditations. Only by making your daily steps in Masonic knowledge and studying the postures, steps and words will you first learn them, and then understand why they are called 'secrets' and why the Craft insists upon their use. This can never be explained in words, so you must learn their meaning by experiment and practice. Just as a successful businessman can never convey the 'secret' of his success to someone without business experience, so the secrets of Masonic progress are learned only by those who actually live them. They are clues to guide your spiritual progress, not confidential communications of secret information.

When you are given the symbolic secrets you should reflect that you are receiving a first lesson in a long course of instruction of an esoteric nature. This knowledge is not taught outside the Lodge, but hidden from public view to help you upon the path into your personal inner life. Having just entered upon that path you will be instructed how to tread it. You have a long journey to reach the goal the Craft opens to you, and that goal is not yet visible. You should absorb instruction slowly and proceed warily and humbly. You have been given a far-off glimpse of the light, but that light will only confound and dazzle you if it is revealed in its fullness before you are ready; Bro. Wilmshurst suggests the well-worn words of Newman's hymn are applicable – 'I do not ask to see the distant scene; one step enough for me'. Remember that the Craft teaches you one step at a time, and each degree in order. If you carry into your daily life what each step signifies and absorb it, you will be become capable of taking the subsequent steps. Traditionally seven years were allocated to the Apprentice Mason to learn his Craft. But the Lecture promises less will suffice if you are found worthy of preferment.

Why does it take seven years? The First Degree of Masonic life is about purification of the body and mind in preparation for the attainment of light in its fullness. Unpurified individuals can never reach that light; their inherent impurities darken their minds and keep them blinded by a self-imposed hoodwink. Purification is needed to eliminate everything in you that clouds your vision and coarsens your nature. This takes time. Bro. Wilmshurst tells us that this 'septenary law' was well known to the Initiates of old and is why seven years are allotted to the work of the First Degree.

You can learn much from the 'word' of the Degree and the posture in which it was imparted, but this must be left to private oral tuition. The directions you were given 'to stand perfectly erect', and the references to 'right [i.e., straight] lines and angles' and 'well-squared actions' comprise a wealth of allusion to secret truths which you should reflect on and inquire into. To an experienced Mason such matters as bodily posture and the 'well-squaring' of your personal actions (even in such minute matters as writing legibly and with every letter well-formed) have a physiological value of great importance in the effort to attain spiritual perfection.

Nature had a purpose in slowly raising man's animal body from a horizontal to an erect posture and transforming his animal passions into moral rectitude, and she has still more to disclose that stems from physiological erectness. 'Unto the upright ariseth light in the darkness,' says the Psalmist, and to Initiates this is literally true. It is a part of your discipline to adopt a physically erect spinal column when engaged in your meditations, as you were taught when making the sign of the degree. That pillar-like stance is known help the attainment of spiritual consciousness or 'light'.

This is why all prayers in the Lodge are said with the Brethren upstanding, with their feet in the posture of the first step and why you were instructed to 'stand perfectly erect' as the light of the 'word' was communicated to you.

Here is a brief hint about the nature of the word of the degree for you to think about. It is said to denote Strength, but perhaps better renderings would be Power, Energy or Ardour, all of which are implied by it. It refers to the energy and ardour with which you should pursue the work of self-perfecting you have begun. The word was given to you because keenness and energy will be the key to your successful progress. All creative work depends upon two interacting active and passive forces, energy and resistance, labour and rest. The Ceremony reminds you that these two forces were represented at the forefront of Solomon's symbolic temple by two 'pillars': i.e., foundation principles. And it is these two principles – activity and contemplation – that you must learn to apply to building your personal temple.

10. Your Testing by the Wardens

After you were entrusted with the secrets you were taken to each Warden in turn and shown how to identify yourself as a Mason. Why was this? It was to check whether you had remembered the instructions and signs that had been communicated to you. The Lodge wants to know that you can reproduce them, so that you don't fail to identify yourself correctly. You were being tested for your capacity to remember and apply what you had been told.

Bro. Wilmshurst says that this is to perpetuate the practices of the Ancient Mysteries and is in accord with scriptural authority and spiritual experience. But I would add that, as a lecturer by trade, I know the best way to check if students have understood what they have been told is to get them to repeat it back; the Craft has been teaching its skills for over six hundred years and has long known how to make sure lessons are learned. You will notice you are told everything three times and then asked to repeat it back three times. This echoes the lecturing maxim: 'Tell what you're going to tell them; tell them; and then tell them what you just told them.' No one should receive knowledge without soon afterwards being put to a test to see if they have understood it.

Bro. Wilmshurst quotes Scripture in support of this view. 'To him that hath shall be given; and from him that hath not shall be taken away even that which he hath.' Remember the severe testing Job was subjected to after acquiring great wealth; remember, too, the Gospels' relation of the 'temptation' or testing episode Jesus underwent immediately after the revelation of spiritual light he experienced at his Jordan baptism.

The testing by the wardens also allows you to translate what you have learned in the Initiation Ceremony into life-experience. You have been introduced to the concept of light and truth so you can expect to be tested as to your worthiness to receive it. In his book *The Imitation of Christ* Thomas à Kempis said, 'He who has not been tested knows nothing'. You cannot hope to internalise a newly discovered truth until you bring it to life under the stress of the temptation to get it wrong.

Earlier in the Ceremony, you will remember that you were conducted to each Warden in turn and had to arouse him from silence. This was to symbolically to demonstrate the need to call into activity the forces latent in yourself. In the second part of the ceremony those same latent forces put you to the test once you start to seek out light and truth. They will question you thus:

Can you retain that light?
Can you exhibit the 'sign' of a true Mason?
Are you striving to tread the path and to take the 'step'?
Do you remember and act upon the 'word' that was given you?
Does your daily life show that you are uttering that word, if not in its completeness, at least in broken syllables or letters?

Our practice of 'halving' or 'lettering' the word is not just precautionary, it is an instructive reminder that, though you might be unable to remember that word in its entirety, if you can at least sound it in stumbling fragmentary efforts, that will let you pass our test.

If you pass, you will be permitted to move on to higher attainments. Sending you round the Wardens to prove yourself a Mason is a dramatic and symbolic representation of that attitude.

11. Your Investiture with an Apron

Each episode of the Ceremony has been structured over the centuries with a psychological accuracy evolved from years of practice and careful adjustment. As you grow in the Craft you will gain many benefits from this form of teaching, and your first Masonic step was passing the test you have just taken.

Once you passed, the Senior Warden reported to the Master that you had made good progress in the science. On hearing this the Master ordered that you be invested with the Apron of an Entered Apprentice Freemason. Now, for the first time, you were entitled to wear the glorious badge of the Order.

Bro. Wilmshurst reminds you of the ancient maxim '*Nullus spiritus sine indumento*', which translates as 'no spirit (or spiritual condition) exists without possessing its appropriate form or garment'. He also suggests you consider a scriptural quotation, from 1 Corinthians 15:38: 'God giveth it a body as it pleaseth Him, and to every seed [or soul] its own body'. This, he tells you, means that, now you have been certified as having attained a new phase of soul-growth, the Master has ordered you to be clothed with a vesture to express your new spiritual condition.

The Masonic Apron is one of the most important and comprehensive of our symbols. Its shape is that of an equilateral triangle, superimposed upon a quadrilateral whose sides are equal (making it a square). The triangle is an ancient and universal emblem of the Spiritual and Formless, whilst the square symbolises the Material Form (or body). A human is a compound of both Spirit and Body, and so the shape of the apron symbolises humanity. The triangle and square are the most ancient ideographs in the world, being the first symbols known ever to have been carved by humans. This means that your Apron can truly be described 'a badge older than that of any other Order in existence'.

Your Apron is made from white lambskin, which is an emblem of purity and innocence. This makes it appropriate clothing for someone freshly born into a Masonic life. It has five points, symbolising the five human senses and other occult truths you will learn about in later degrees. If you add the three sides of its triangular part to the four of its quadrangular, you get seven, the number corresponding with the colours in the spectrum, the notes of the musical scale and the days of the week. If you multiply those same numbers, you get twelve, the number of the zodiacal signs through which our solar system moves and which are reflected in the twelve Hebrew tribes and the twelve Apostles.

As you advance through the Degrees and perhaps join the higher ranks of the Masonic Hierarchy, at each step your will see a corresponding change in the form and colours of your Apron. The sacred or royal colours – blue, purple and scarlet – will be added to the white lambskin, and ornaments of silver and gold will be added. These elaborations are intended to symbolise the progress of the wearer, and should point to the unfolding of spiritual graces from the depths of inward advancement. As the strength of your central spirit grows, so your Apron should reflect that growth with symbolic rosettes, celestial blue borders and ornaments of silver. If you continue to advance, the pale azure will deepen to royal blue, and the silver turn to gold. When you become a Master Mason your Apron will boast a fastener in the form of a serpent, a symbol of Wisdom, to indicate that wisdom with which your whole organism has been devised.

So, newly dressed Brother, your Apron is a symbol of yourself, and, with progression, its growing beauty will reflect a corresponding growth of spirituality in your life. Treat your Apron with the same respect you do your soul. Never treat it with levity or entrust it to any hands but your own. It should be respected as the outward image of your inward self.

Bro. Wilmshurst reminds us that in the New Testament, Matthew 32:1–14, it says that no man may enter heaven without wearing a 'wedding garment' and likens it to the rule that no Mason may enter a Lodge without wearing the Apron that proclaims his amity with the universal Craft. But you do not need to restrict the use of your Apron to the Lodge. You should visualise yourself clothed in it at all times, whether or not you actually wear it. Some Brethren wear their Masonic clothing in private to conduct their personal meditations. And some hold it in such regard that they ask to wear their Apron in the grave.

12. The Charge in the North-East Corner

After donning your Apron you were placed in the North-East corner of the Lodge. At one time the word lodge did not refer to the room in which the Ceremony took place but to the Lodge Tracing Board for the degree being worked. In preserving this tradition the Lodge of Living Stones arranges for that board to be placed in the North-East corner of the temple, and your feet are placed in the form a right angle to frame that board.

The North-East corner is a point of great symbolic importance. It is where the North of the lodge, the realm of darkness, meets the East of the lodge, the realm of light. It symbolises your condition. You stand on that cusp and can either step onward to the light of the East, or retreat to the darkness of the North; only you can decide which direction your life will take. It is also the direction from where the sun rises on the day of greatest light.

You are encouraged by the ritual to renew your spiritual activity and think of your personality as a 'foundation stone', which is the basis for raising a 'superstructure'. This implies more than just character building. In the past candidates have been told to build not a superstructure but a 'castle in the air', a term which referred to an 'airy', ethereal or spiritual body: 'a house not made with hands nor subject to decay, but eternal and heavenly'.

This metaphysical symbolism is a subject for your private reflection and tuition, but remember your mortal, visible body has been built up gradually, cell by cell and tissue by tissue, out of the life forces of Nature, so you have within yourself the capacity to evolve an immortal invisible 'superstructure', an 'airy' castle or fortress, where your conscious soul can retreat when its earthly vesture falls away. The erection of this superstructure is known in Masonic mysticism as 'building King Solomon's Temple', and it is something that you, like every Mason, must build for yourself.

During the ritual charge you were reminded of your duty to Charity. But do not think that this duty will be fulfilled simply by giving money to those who are financially poor, distressed or deserving. The words of the ritual may seem to suggest that it does, but remember the ritual is a veil, and it masks deeper truths than its surface words show.

The 'Charity' you are so earnestly encouraged to cultivate would perhaps be better expressed by the term 'compassion'. This includes Love, which is a synonym for Charity, but it embraces much more. 'Charity', in its Latin original *Caritas*, meant 'dearness', and your Masonic duty is to regard all creatures in a spirit of universal and impartial dearness, as pilgrims upon a single path. Whilst others may be at different stages of development, all are evolving towards a common goal. In their struggles to work out that destiny, whether they thank you for your help or not, it remains your duty to give them all the compassion and help you can.

Material gifts are the lowest form of giving. Giving mental and moral succour is of greater value, because it improves the mental nature of its recipient. Giving from the heart is a sacrificial outpouring of your spirit, which is the highest form of giving. This is the Charity you are urged to practice. Work at it and you will quicken the life of all around you and send forth leaves from your own tree of life for the healing of the nations. At the Centre of your personal system dwells a sun, clouded though it may by the fogs and mists of your own making. Like the solar orb in Nature it can send forth its beneficent radiation persistently, unstintingly and impartially to the whole world. It is for you, as a new Initiate, to make it visible.

Think about the philosophy of giving, and why it is better to give than to receive. Humanity is often selfish, grasping and acquisitive. All your days you have been receiving, from nature, from your parents and from society. This has encouraged you to become egocentric. You have been trained to secure yourself a living and a professional position. But, as a Mason seeking Initiation, you are impelled by forces within yourself to rise beyond Nature and submit to a law higher than selfish acquisitiveness. All your energies need to be reversed. Getting must give way to giving.

Bro. Wilmshurst quotes Matthew Arnold:

Know, man is all that Nature is but more,
And in that 'more' lie all his hopes of good.

From that 'more' you build a 'superstructure' upon the foundation of your old self – not by getting and receiving but through giving of yourself. The more you give, the more you eventually receive. All energy is conserved and returns to its source, enriched by the contacts it makes in its passage.

From the ritual you learn that self-giving is the foundation stone of the Masonic life. Charity has its degrees and may be practised in many ways, the highest of which is the habitual pouring forth of compassionate love to all. Those who have freely received must as freely give. By your Initiation, you have been offered the blessing of light and understanding. You are required never to withhold that light from anyone who asks it from you.

The most moving moment of the Ceremony came when, pauperised and denuded of everything valuable, you were invited to make a gift to your poor and distressed fellow-creatures. From what resources could you possibly make any gift? Only from the contents of your heart. If it is empty you have nothing to give. If it is filled with love you can give yourself.

13. The Working Tools

It is one thing to advise you *what* to do to promote your advancement, but by now you must have been wondering *how* you do it. This is why the ritual gives you guidance on self-discipline and self-improvement, which are referred to as 'working tools'.

There are three working tools, and their mystical significance was explained on their presentation. They are not just emblems to be ignored or forgotten. They represent duties that are essential to your Masonic progress, and you are intended to use them daily.

The measuring gauge helps you allocate your time to the performance of three distinct duties. They do not involve equal expenditure of time, but each duty has equal value. It teaches:

> A duty to work with the Divine Plan of The Great Architect and to study spiritual things,
>
> A duty to yourself, to satisfy your material needs and take care of your family, and
>
> An altruistic duty to those less happily placed than yourself.

Together these duties form an equilateral triangle, each of which is as important as the other two. Indeed the equal-sided triangle is an ancient symbol of the Deity, and if you see it as signifying that the Divine Plan, yourself and your neighbour form a unity, then you see how each part is a necessary support to both the others.

As a Mason you must find a way to balance your performance of these three duties, to make them form a matched, equal-sided triangle. You are expected to pay equal attention to spiritual matters, to yourself and to your neighbour. Remember, undue stress on any one of them will not maintain a true balance. That is why you are told that, when giving altruistic help to your neighbour, you should 'not do so unless you can do it without detriment to yourself or your connections'. When you first hear these words they sound contrary to the spirit of self-sacrifice, but there is great wisdom in them. You can only serve and help another if you have first made yourself competent to serve. 'Self-love is not so vile a sin as self-neglect,' as Shakespeare says. There are many people who fail to improve themselves but try to improve others. Selfishness will disappear if your devotion is habitually accorded to what is higher than yourself – and that in turn will qualify you to help your neighbour.

As you progress you will learn of other working tools in other Degrees, but they will not help you if you do not start by using those of the First Degree. You are advised to pay attention to them until their performance becomes automatic. And you will find your education greatly helped if you make time for a systematic reading of literature dealing with Masonic and related subjects. 'Reading is good prayer,' says Bro. Wilmshurst, provided it is of a kind that helps your quest for light. Masonry is a work of the mind, so any study that helps to expand of your mental faculties is a 'working tool' and opens fresh doors of perception for you.

14. The Tracing Board

The last information you should be given is an explanation of the Tracing Board, but this is often deferred to another occasion, since it is a long piece of ritual.

You will have noticed that you have been instructed in spiritual and ethical matters. Now the Tracing Board speaks to your intellectual nature. It teaches esoteric knowledge of a philosophical nature. Esoteric information means the sort that is not imparted outside the Lodge nor taught by churches and other systems of public instruction. It is a form of teaching reserved for advanced tuition and is hidden in symbolic pictures. At one time these cryptic designs were drawn upon the floor of the Lodge by the Initiating Master when needed. They were washed away by the Candidate at the close of the Ceremony.

In the official Lecture of the First Degree the new Mason is recommended 'to seek a Master and from him gain instruction'. This is an age-old practice of a junior Brother seeking out and attaching himself for seven years to an expert Master so as to gain private tuition fuller than that possible in Lodge meetings. The relationship of Master and Apprentice originated in the Trade Guilds and later became a common business practice. Originally, though, it was a duty the Master undertook for the *spiritual* training of his neotype. This practice is widely followed in the East and was always observed in the Mysteries of antiquity. Today few Masters are competent to teach, so that few Candidates learn what lies beneath the surface of the Craft doctrine.

But where the true relationship of Master and Disciple does exist it is an intimate and precious spiritual tie with reciprocal responsibility. Bro. Wilmshurst reminds us of an old maxim, 'when the pupil is ready the Master will be found waiting', and that such a Master will impart personal instruction of a deeper and wider character than can be given publicly.

Finally, as the ceremony ended you were told to retire from the Lodge to be restored to what were called your 'personal comforts'. These were the clothing and belongings you surrendered before entering the lodge; within the Lodge such possessions have no value. A pointed lesson lies in your being directed to resume them. From now on it will be your duty to reassess your opinion of their value and, using them for what they are worth, you will learn to discriminate between what is transient and what is enduring. What you have hitherto clung to as 'comforts' you may come to find irksome discomforts as you acquire a balanced understanding that looks beyond comfort or discomfort.

The **'Ancient Charge'** with which the Ceremony concludes is self-explanatory, and I will not discuss it here. It is not an integral part of the Ceremony, but it differs in method and language. The Ceremony proper is 'veiled in allegory' and contains cryptic phrases and sub-surface allusions at every turn. The 'Ancient Charge' has no ulterior meaning. It is a simple homily compliment-ing the Candidate upon his reception into the Order and informing him of observances with which he will be expected to comply.

The Charge embodies advice formerly given to young men becoming apprenticed to the Operative Building Guilds, enjoining them to good citizenship and to lead a moral and useful life. But present-day Candidates for Speculative Masonry will have been checked to ensure they possess these qualifications before joining the Craft, so the Charge simply perpetuates an old custom of the Trade Guilds on admitting an Apprentice to membership and should be enjoyed as such.

CONCLUSION

To sum up, this is what the Ceremony is for. The first half is designed to offer the spiritual light desired by a Candidate who seeks truth from his heart and comes prepared in mind and person to receive it. The second and complementary half is meant to teach the Candidate how to retain and increase that light, so as never to relapse into darkness.

When you were being initiated you were given an first glimpse of supra-natural light. It rests with you to prove worthy of it and to enlarge that temporary glimpse into a permanent vision. In a few swift episodes the Ceremony dramatises the 'Apprentice' stage of the spiritual life. It explains how the light of a spiritual Sun burns and blazes at your centre and has appeared above your conscious horizon to manifest in ever-increasing power. As that Sun rises higher and higher within you, so your inner darkness will be dispelled and your materialism spiritualised. As Bro. Wilmshurst puts it 'If thine eye [soul] be single [simple and unadulterated by passion and wrong notions], thy whole being will be full of light'.

You are taught that light will show you that underlying all things is the Sacred Law. That Law comprises physical, moral and ultra-physical aspects, and the roots of your being are integrated into it. As you learn to unify your personal will with the Universal Will and harmonize your mind with the Cosmic Prototype, you will become a conscious collaborator with it. Love is a means of fulfilling the Law, so you are encouraged to cultivate boundless charity and compassion towards all beings. As Bro. Wilmshurst puts it, *tout aimer, c'est tout comprendre*: 'to love everything is to understand everything'.

The Apprentice stage of Masonry is one of purification, education and self-control. No amount of book learning or instruction can teach you what you can learn only by your own experience. Even these notes are but an elementary preface to deeper aspects of Initiation which you will only learn by living them. To tell the fuller truths about the subject would scare and discourage, rather than enlighten and help. For this reason our science is a veiled and secret one.

If you wish to progress, never gauge what you find within the Lodge by the same standard as you apply to the outside world. Many Brethren go wrong through lack of humility and willingness to learn. They look at matters of the inner life with the eyes of the outer world. They question their ideas about Masonry to see how far they can adapt it to other beliefs they hold, and they seek to apply worldly wisdom to a knowledge not of this world. Masonry requires a special education and the training of a sense which in the present state of human evolution is far from common. Spiritual things must be spiritually discerned.

When you enter the Lodge in search of light you should leave all your previous learning behind with your garments and loose the shoes of personal opinion from off your feet. You should become as a child being taken into a world of new ideas and a different logic from the one you have known. You must recast your ideas and life. Will your pride allow you to?

If it will not, you will continue to shroud your inner light, and the Craft will teach you nothing of value, whatever titular rank you may attain. If it will, then you will become an Initiate in fact as well as in name and find your eyes opening to a depth of truth of which you are at present unconscious.

In the Mysteries of old the Candidate, because of his new birth into light, was spoken of as a 'little child'. Casting aside all your knowledge and reducing yourself to the docility and single-mindedness of infancy does not fit the modern mindset. Nonetheless, these qualities are indispensable to a Candidate for Wisdom. It is not the learned, the critical or the worldly wise who are suffered to come to the light: it is the little children

Appendix

The following notes were written by W.L. Wilmshurst to help Masons who had recently taken their First Degree to understand the deeper implications of Freemasonry. They will also, perhaps, help other Brethren who wish to better understand the purpose and the meaning of the Initiation Ceremony. They were originally written as Lodge Paper No. 16 of the Lodge of Living Stones and published by J.M. Watkins in 1932

LODGE PAPER NO. 16

THE LODGE OF LIVING STONES,

No. 4957.

The Ceremony of Initiation.

Analysis and Commentary.

BY

W.L. WILMSHURST, P.M.,
P.A.G.D.C. (England)
and P.P.G.W. (West Yorks.)

1932.
Privately Printed.

J.M. WATKINS,. 21 Cecil Court, Charing Cross Road,. London, W.C. 2.

INTRODUCTION

I

The endeavour is to indicate the reason for the existence of the Masonic system, to draw aside the veil of allegory and symbolism in which the Initiation Ceremony is clothed, and to reveal its spirit and sub-surface significance.

The First Degree Ceremony used on the reception of a Candidate into the Craft is designed to introduce him to the first stage of a system of knowledge and self-discipline which, if faithfully followed up and lived out in his personal life, will clarify and transform his mind from its natural state of darkness to one of Light, i.e., expanded clear-seeing spiritual consciousness raised far beyond, and existing independently of, the perceptions of the natural senses. It is, therefore, called a Ceremony of Initiation (from *in ire* to go inwards, i.e., beyond the merely material surfaces of things), and because it is meant to mark the beginning (*initium*) of a new order of personal life and consciousness. It might equally well be called one of Regeneration or Rebirth; indeed its parallel in Religion is the sacrament of Baptism, which is the initial incident of the religious life and is performed at the West end of a Church, just as a Masonic Candidate enters the Lodge and begins his Masonic career in the symbolic West. It is a ceremony provided to give an answer to what the Candidate professes to be the predominant wish of his heart – a wish well expressed by probably the oldest prayer in the world, which is still used daily by millions of our fellowmen in the East:-

> *From the unreal lead me to the Real;*
> *From the darkness lead me to Light;*
> *From the mortal bring me to Immortality!*

The presence or absence of this aspiration in a Candidate should be the test of his fitness for Initiation. Any less exalted motive for seeking Initiation falls short of the true intention. The Candidate's attitude should be one of definite intelligent expectation of spiritual good to come to him, and of positive aspiration and heart-hunger for it; equally definitely, it must not be for any material or social advantage, nor a merely negative state of curiosity or uncertainty as to what is to be found in the Craft.

II

For every Candidate the Initiation Ceremony implies that whatever academic or scientific learning he possesses, whatever philosophical ideas he holds, whatever religious creed he professes, prior to Initiation, there remains something more – indeed something vastly more – for him yet to learn and to which the Craft can help to lead him. This does not mean that he will necessarily discover his previous convictions to be false; on the other hand, so far as they be true he will find abundant confirmation and implication of them and, so far as they are erroneous or imperfect, he will learn to modify them. It means that he must be prepared to find some of his wonted, and perhaps even most deeply rooted, ideas to be apprehensions of Truth so partial and limited that they operate as obstructions to the wider vision which might be his, and that the more tenaciously he clings to them, the more he may be blocking his own light. If, therefore, he is to profit by the Light to which the Craft leads, he must be prepared to keep his mind open and fluid and to make such mental self-surrender as occasion warrants. We all tend to feel so certain of ourselves, so wise in our own conceits, and too often are unaware that we have much to unlearn before we can become truly teachable. But from earliest times the Candidate for Initiation has been called a "child" and taught to regard himself as such.

Accordingly the divesting of the Candidate's person prior to the Ceremony is symbolic of the mental unclothing required of him, whilst his self-abandonment to be taken wherever he is led and to do whatever he is told betokens the meekness and docility with which his mind should follow Truth wherever it may lead, even into apparently perilous places and among ideas not recognised by the conventions and orthodoxies of the world without. For true Initiation involves a spiritual adventure, a voyage of the mind, not into the unknowable but into what the Candidate has never yet known or experienced; and it leads to regions where he travels farthest who carries least burdens, where he acquires most who casts away most of himself, and where the really heart hungry are increasingly filled with good things from which the intellectually rigid and the rich in conventional knowledge are automatically precluded. To the single-minded, Wisdom has ways of revealing itself which the learned understand not.

Mental self-tripping and readjustment is, of course, not a sudden, but a gradual process. No Candidate is called upon to do undue or too sudden violence to himself, but rather to adapt himself gradually to the new conditions and to become transformed by a slow but steady renewing of his mind and outlook. See how this is evidenced by his progressive unclothing as he passes on from Degree to Degree! In the First only certain parts of his person are bared; in the Second, only certain other and complementary parts. It is not until the Third Degree that the maximum unclothing is called for, by that time he is presumed to be inured to self-surrender and better able to make the larger sacrifice which that sublime Degree involves.

III

To turn now to the Ceremony itself. Up to about the year 1700 formally compiled Rituals did not exist. The working was transmitted orally. There was no such thing as a memorised form, mechanically repeated with such word perfection and dignified elocution as may be, but an extempore pronouncement of real power and spiritual efficacy, performed by a Master possessing complete understanding of what he did, and able to adapt or amplify the ceremony in accordance with the culture, intelligence and probable requirements of a properly prepared Candidate. The actual form of words employed was (and still always is) the least important element about the Ceremony. What is of far vaster consequence is the ability of the Initiator, and those co-operating with him, to infuse into it such spiritual fervour and emotional momentum that what is done and said over the Candidate shall penetrate his heart and mind, and awaken certain truths in his soul, – a result requiring, as its first condition, that the Candidate be a fit and proper person and properly prepared for it.

Even today, the Irish and many Continental Masonic Constitutions work to no set ritual. Certain traditional landmarks and age-old usages are uniformly observed, but for the rest (e.g. the various charges, explanations and entrustings) the wording of the Ceremony is left to the inspiration and emotion of the moment.

The Ritual which, with slight local variations, has become traditional with us embodies all these landmarks and usages and has been compiled with extraordinary and, indeed, inspired skill and wisdom. To treat it superficially, or regard it as a composition to be reeled off one's memory in a "non-stop" fashion, is to miss the purport and the beauties of a highly complex and comprehensive compilation. Analysis of it shows that it is built up of fourteen distinct "movements" or episodes, in two series of seven each.

The first series is associated with the Candidate's state of darkness; it is an ascending or crescendo series rising, like an emotional wave, to a climax at the moment of his symbolic restoration to Light. The second series is associated with the state of Light to which he has been lifted up; it is a descending or diminuendo series dealing with matters consequent upon his attainment of Light; the emotional billow, as it were, dies gradually away, but leaving the Candidate's being flooded with new perceptions and stimulated by a quickening influence such as he never previously knew and which will probably take him some time to assimilate.

The sequence of these episodes is as follows; and they will indicate what a large range of ideas has been compressed within a short Ceremony:

STATE OF DARKNESS
1. The Admission to the Lodge.
2. The Prayer of Dedication.
3. The Mystical Journey (or Perambulation).
4. The Declarations of Freedom, Motive, and Perseverance.
5. The Advance from W. to E.
6. The Obligation.
7. The Restoration to Light.

STATE OF LIGHT
8. The Revelation of the Greater and Lesser Lights.
9. The Entrustment with the Secrets.
10. The Testing by the Wardens.
11. The Investiture with the Clothing.
12. The Instruction in the N.E.
13. The Instruction in the Working Tools.
14. The Instruction in the Tracing Board.

Each of these fourteen incidents provides scope for prolonged reflection and comment, but in these notes only brief observations can be made upon each of them in succession.

The separation of the Ceremony into two main sub-divisions, the "state of Darkness" and the "state of Light", has a far-reaching allusiveness: first to cosmic truth and in relation to human life generally; secondly, historically and in correspondence with the Ancient Mysteries.

Cosmically, all human life begins its quest for Light and Truth in a state of darkness as our nature, our purpose and destiny. We are, as it were, born blind or hoodwinked about them; as the Ancients taught, we have all drunk the cup of Lethe and the water of forgetfulness before descending to birth in the flesh. Our quest, therefore, at the outset of our earthly career must necessarily be a darkened one, a mere hoodwinked fumbling about for we know not what, until the pains, sorrows and disillusionments of existence awake us to the fact that we are wasting our substance among shadows and futilities, and that there may be something higher and better worth hunting for. This preliminary condition of mind and soul the Initiates likened to being in a place which they called "the Hall of Ignorance" or "the Hall of Truth in Darkness", in which we grope about for a Light and Wisdom which are at all times around us, but which we cannot find because our faculties are as yet sealed from perceiving them.

Later on, when experience has caused a man to turn away in distaste from outer interests to the quest of better things, he becomes initiated in to the science of them, and was said to have entered the "Hall of Learning" or the "Hall of Truth in Light", for by this time he is no longer ignorantly groping in the dark, but has become actuated by a definite and enlightened resolve to find the Reality behind the shadows.

It is these two conditions, one of groping ignorantly and with blinded eyes for the Reality behind temporal existence, and one of seeking it intelligently and with the opened eyes of the Initiate, that are reproduced in the two subdivisions of our First Degree Ceremony. There remains a third condition, but for the novice it is as yet a long way off and is, therefore, beyond the purview of our present enquiry; its attainment is described as entering the "Hall of Wisdom", which is possible only to Master Masons who have passed beyond the two previous "Halls" and whose search has been rewarded with finding the ultimate secrets of life.

Preceding the actual Ceremony, however, there is implied a preliminary and very necessary routine, – the due Preparation of the Candidate, some remarks upon which must preface our commentary upon the fourteen points of the Ceremony itself

As to the sources of the Ceremony, it (as also the official E.A. Lecture and Tracing Board Explanation provided to interpret it) is a blend of various streams of influence. The chief of these is the traditional method – usually called the "Secret Doctrine" – common to all the Ancient Mysteries and Initiation systems from the dawn of history: a method and doctrine always held in reserve from the knowledge of the masses of the people, constituting stronger "meat" and imparting deeper truths than the more simple instruction, or "milk", provided for the general public by the current education and religious institutions of a given time or place. As is well known to students of the history of religion, behind the exoteric doctrine of every great Teacher or religious Founder, has always existed an esoteric counterpart of it for advanced disciples.

Combined with elements of this ancient esoteric wisdom are elements from more recent cognate systems, such as Hermeticism, the Hebrew Cabala, and Rosicrucianism, as also survivals from mediaeval Gild Masonry, whilst the Holy Scriptures which have served to nourish the religious life of the West are interfused with all these and act as a unifying and explanatory "great light".

Accordingly we find our Masonic Ritual, as the offspring of these sources, continually using the language of its parents, speaking now in the terms or symbols of one and now in those of another of them; and it becomes clear that all these sources have been stewards of the same Mysteries, that they proclaim the same truth and mean the same thing, and can be constantly cross-referenced and found to be mutually interpretative.

Take one of a host of possible examples – the Preparation of the Candidate. The Craft requires every Candidate for Initiation to come "properly prepared". In Religion this is paralleled by the Church requiring its neophytes to be "prepared" for Confirmation into fuller realisation of spiritual life. And every ancient and modern Initiation system has required it; indeed the preparation insisted on in antiquity and in more advanced secret Orders than the Craft, was, and still is, of an extremely intensive character. But the point to be stressed here is that, for those who really desire Light, a preliminary orientation of will, heart and mind is indispensable to their desire becoming fulfilled, and "Prepare ye the way of the Lord!" is the Biblical confirmation of what the Ancient Mysteries required and what the Craft still inculcates. And when, with us, the Master of the Lodge dispatches his Deacon to prepare the Candidate for his reception, is he not still echoing and giving a personal value to the words of impersonal and cosmic application. "Behold, I will send my messenger to prepare the way before me"?

IV

The mental preparation of the Candidate should have been proceeding for a considerable time before the Ceremony is conferred. It can be considerably assisted by his Masonic sponsors, upon whom rests the responsibility of vouching for his fitness for Initiation, and who in private converse can adumbrate to him a broad idea of what is involved and assure themselves of his sympathetic response to it.

As to the symbolic preparation of his external person, much closer attention is paid to this in Continental Lodges than is usual with us. He is taken to a quiet ante-room and there left alone for some time to compose his mind and read some sentences warning him of the solemnity of his project and the desirability of proceeding with it in a spirit of meekness and confidence or of withdrawing from it while there is yet time.

After an interval he is interviewed by the Deacon and asked for his decision. If he desires to proceed he is then asked to write brief replies to some such questions as these:—

(1) What is your view of the purpose of human life and the nature of human destiny?
(2) What is your object in seeking to be initiated?
(3) What may the Craft hope to receive from you in return for what you expect to receive from it?

He is left to write his replies, which are then taken into the Lodge and submitted to the Master's approval, who declares whether they are satisfactory, in which event only the ballot is taken. Upon his election the Deacon is despatched to greet the Candidate with the tidings and to invite him to surrender his metals and money. After which the formal preparation of his person proceeds as with us; this being done with solemnity, the reason for each separate act of preparation being briefly explained by the Deacon.

It were well if the above practice or an approximation of it were always followed. In any event, great importance attaches to the due performance of the Deacon's ministrations so as to create the most favourable mental conditions for the Candidate before he enter the Lodge. (The symbolic value of the Deacon's work is explained in our Lodge Paper No. 4, and it is in the spirit of that explanation that he should discharge his duties).

If it be essential that the Candidate should enter the Lodge properly prepared, it is equally important that those waiting to receive and initiate him should themselves be prepared in heart and intention to do so. Even the atmosphere of the Temple should be prepared by rendering it peaceful and free of commotion. The W.M. can ensure this by enjoining complete silence during the interval preceding the Candidate's entrance and inviting the Brethren to reflect upon the nature of the work in hand and to unite with him in earnest aspiration that that work may be spiritually effectual.

The unofficiating Brethren present are not meant to be mere spectators of the Ceremony. The whole Lodge, and not only the acting officials of it, should participate in the mystery. Great is the power of united concentrated thought and intention in impressing a Candidate's mentality and awaking it to new and spiritual perceptions – and to this end the spoken work of the Master and Officers actively concerned can be very greatly assisted by the silent mental co-operation of the unofficiating Brethren.

PART I

1. – The Admission

From the place of preparation the Candidate is led to the door of the Lodge. This he finds close tyled. He "meets with opposition" (as the E.A. Lecture says) and cannot gain admission save in the prescribed way.

In other words, on turning from the world without to the world within, his first discovery is to find his way blocked by an intervening barrier. What is that barrier? What does the door of the Lodge symbolise?

Obviously it symbolises some obstructive element in himself. He is made to recognise that any opposition to his own spiritual advancement comes from within himself and must be overcome by his own efforts. (Hence it is that the Candidate is required to give the knocks himself; they should never be given for him by any one else.)

The purport of this episode is expressly declared in the E.A. Lecture to be subjective and mystical. The knocks are there stated to be interpretable in the light of the Scriptural direction, "Ask and ye shall have; Seek and ye shall find; Knock and it shall be opened to you." This threefold direction, observe, not only corresponds with the triple knocks, but also with the triple faculties of the Candidate himself. He should "ask" with the prayerful aspirations of his heart; he should "seek" with the intellectual activities of his mind; he should "knock" with the force of his bodily energies. He who hopes to find the Light within must devote his entire being to the quest; it demands and engages the attention of the whole man.

How true to life and to psychology is this symbolic opposition at the door of the Lodge! We all erect our mental barriers. The habitual thought-methods, prejudices, preconceptions and "fixed ideas" in which we indulge in the course of life in the outer world, become obstructions to the perception of things of the world within. They create mental deposits which condense and harden, until they obscure the wider, deeper, clearer vision we might have, but for own self-created limitations. We erect and tyle our own door against ourselves and block our own light, and eventually, on seeking to turn to the Light, find ourselves confronted by darkness and opposition of our own creating. And it is just these barriers that must be broken down by our own efforts and the force of our own persistent "knocks".

For "knocks" it may be helpful to think of a more modern term – vibrations. Persistent vibrations in a given direction will, as is well known, eventually break down whatever is opposed to them, whether physical or mental. Vibrations of faith remove mountains. Vibrations of intellectual energy result in the solution of problems. Vibrations of emotion break through into the hearts of others. Vibration of spiritual aspiration penetrate into higher worlds and open doors into them. And all this is signified by the simple incident of the Candidate meeting with opposition at the door of the Lodge and gaining admission as the result of his own symbolic knocks.

2. – The Prayer of Dedication

The initial act of the Ceremony is appropriately a prayer by the assembled Brethren:
 (1) That the Candidate (who has already been elected to formal membership of the Craft) may now become *spiritually* incorporated into the Great Brotherhood, and
 (2) For his endowment with such an influx of **wisdom** as, by virtue of that incorporation, will give him increasing **power** to manifest the **beauty** of holiness.

The brevity and simplicity of this prayer are liable to obscure its deep implications. Observe (from the three words just emboldened above) that it contains the first unobtrusive reference to that trinity of Wisdom, Strength and Beauty of which the Candidate will hear later on, and of which it is prayed that he may become a living manifestation.

Note too, that there is no reference in the prayer to morality of merely ethical virtues; it invokes something far loftier than these – the gift of the Spirit; it strikes a keynote intended to govern the tone of both the Ceremony and the Candidate's whole after-life.

Observe, too, that it is not a prayer **by** the Candidate (who is required only to "kneel and listen" to it), but one **for** him and for the Craft itself; it is a prayer that the spiritual efficiency of the whole Fraternity may become augmented by this new accession to it. Every Brother present, therefore, should unite with the Chaplain in a strong tension of aspiration that the prayer may become realised in the joint interests of both the Craft and its new member. Later on, the latter should make the prayer his own, remembering throughout his life that it was once offered over him in his darkness and helplessness on behalf of the whole Craft, and that it falls to himself to justify increasingly the invocation then so solemnly made in his behalf.

3. – The Perambulation or Mystical Journeying

Next follows the Perambulation. But this preceded by an inquiry to the Candidate: where does he repose reliance in circumstances of danger and difficulty? It is obvious that he is about to be exposed to circumstances of that character, and the question is therefore put to ascertain whether he ought to be allowed to expose himself to them or not. The answer to the question should always be his own and should spring spontaneously from his own mind and lips; to prompt him with an answer detracts from the reality of the Ceremony and encourages him to give a reply which may be insincere. The Ceremony implies that if he cannot voluntarily give the proper response to the question, he is unfit for Initiation and should be led back out of the Lodge. If, on the other hand, he responds satisfactorily, well and good; the Ceremony may proceed and will be a test of the Candidate's profession of faith.

What **are** the dangers and difficulties he is about to be exposed to? In our Ceremony they are, of course, merely theoretic and symbolic. But in the Initiation Rites of the Ancient Mysteries (of which ours are a faint echo) they were extremely exacting, realistic and affrighting, and such as put a Candidate to severe tests of mental stability and moral fitness. They may be read about more fully in literature on the subject, from which it will be gathered how very essential it was that a Candidate for Initiation into the secrets and mysteries of his own being should possess not only a stable faith and moral centre, but also a sound mind in a sound body. Otherwise grave responsibility rested upon both the Initiators and the Candidate, and grave risks of damage to the latter's reason attached by suffering an unfit person to "rashly run forward" towards experiences for which he was unsuited.

Hence it is that a Candidate is still called upon to make a public declaration of faith and to be passed in review before the Lodge ere the Ceremony is proceeded with, so that his Initiators may be satisfied of his fitness.

This is the first reason for the ceremonial Perambulation. But there is another, of equal importance. The journey round the Lodge is a symbolic representation of the Candidate's own life-journeyings in this world prior to his request for Initiation into the world within. The dangers and difficulties referred to are the vicissitudes encountered in his own personal Odyssey; indeed the wanderings and buffetings of Odysseus are an ancient poetic allegory of these experiences, of a like character to the parable of the career of the Prodigal Son before he "came to himself" and struck the true path.

We must observe two most noteworthy details in connection with this symbolic journey. The first is that, though in a state of darkness himself, he is not alone, but has with him an enlightened guide. Moreover he is compassed about by a cloud of witnesses keenly anxious for his spiritual advancement and restoration to light. The significance of this detail is that every traveller through life has within himself his own invisible guide, and that his soul's upward struggles are observed by many unseen watchers.

The second is that in the course of his symbolic journey he is led to each Warden in turn, whom, by a particular gesture, he as it were arouses from silence and stirs to utterance. The gesture itself is in fact a repetition of the knocks previously given at the door of the Lodge. But whereas those knocks were first addressed to inert material (the door), they are now applied to a living being (the Warden). What does this imply? It signifies that in our efforts to turn away from the outer world and penetrate to the Light of the inner one, we not only overcome our own self-created opposition, but we awaken and stimulate into activity certain living but hitherto dormant energies within ourselves.

Of those latent energies with him the Candidate will come to learn more later. Suffice it for the moment to know that his desire for Light awakens real but as yet slumbering potencies within himself, which from now onwards will become stimulated and promote his spiritual advancement. In each of us reside certain dormant principles (represented by the two Wardens) higher than the normal benighted human reason knows;[1] it is these which it is possible to provoke into activity, and which, then awakened, no longer block our passage but speed a man on his ways with, as it were, the mystical greeting: "Pass, Good Report!"

The expression "Good Report" is a modern form of a very ancient mystical title accorded to the Candidate. It means much more than "good reputation" in the popular sense of the phrase. It implies that the Candidate's nature is one animated by spiritual sincerity, one that rings true like a coin, and that sounds forth a convincing note when it speaks. "True of voice" was the Egyptian form of "Good Report", and it is for this reason that, on approaching each Warden, our present Candidates are called upon to sound forth

---

[1] These latent spiritual principles in man, symbolised by the Wardens or "Watchmen", are frequently referred to in the V.S.L: e.g. "I have set watchmen upon thy walls which shall never hold their peace day nor night" (Isaiah 62: 8); "Unless the Lord keep the city the watchman waketh but in vain" (Psalms 127: 1).

own note so that the Warden may determine whether they are indeed "true of voice" and qualified to be passed on.

"**Say** something that I may **see** you," said Socrates to a shy youth who sought his instruction, for a man's speech betrayeth him to the sensitive ear, which is able to judge of the speaker's sincerity and spiritual status. And hence it is that the Candidate is required to sound forth his own voice to the Wardens.

4. – The Professions of Freedom, Motive, and Perseverance

After both Wardens have assured themselves of the Candidate's fitness for advancement to the East, he is so certified and presented to the Master for Initiation. But, before the Master accepts him, the Candidate is required to pledge himself to three requirements:

(1) That he seeks the Light voluntarily, for its own sake, and from no unworthy or material motive.

(2) That his objects in seeking it are two-fold:
  i. knowledge for himself, and
  ii. a desire to make himself, in virtue of that knowledge, of more extensive service to humanity.

(3) That he will persevere in the path about to be disclosed to him (which means perseverance not merely through the formal Ceremony, but in pursuing throughout his subsequent daily life all that that Ceremony typifies).

It is important that these questions, too, should be answered spontaneously and without prompting. For they involve definite personal commitments of a far-reaching character to which no one should be suffered to pledge himself lightly or under persuasion.

Especially noteworthy is the second promise – that such higher knowledge as he acquires shall be used in human service. Now, no one can truly serve humanity until he knows how to do so; a good deal of activity is displayed nowadays that passes by the name of service, but is not such enlightened or sanctified service as is meant by the Craft; therefore the acquisition of special knowledge is mentioned first, so that the Candidate may learn how to serve really and effectually; but, when acquired, that knowledge is not to be for selfish purposes but to be put to selfless service of the race. The enlightenment of Initiation is not to be for his private benefit only; it must become of importance to, and a trust for, the general good. Every real Initiate, by the mere fact of his enlightenment, becomes so much salt and seasoning to a corrupting world; hence he is called upon not to hide his light but to use it and let it shine before men, that they may see in him an example worth following.

Service, indeed, is and ever has been the ulterior motive of the Mysteries; but there are many forms of it, and service can be rendered in quite other and higher ways than ordinary altruistic activity. Of these the Candidate will learn more later. But let him never forget that, at the threshold of his Masonic life, he pledged himself to become a servant of humanity

5. – The Advance from West to East

This is a small episode, yet one of far-reaching significance.

The Candidate has just completed symbolic Odyssean journeying around the Lodge, which exemplifies his benighted life wanderings since he came to birth in this world (the "West"). During his career he has passed blindly, yet never without unseen guidance, through regions and experiences sometimes of darkness (the "North"), sometimes of less or greater enlightenment (the "South", "West" and "East"), yet entirely ignorant whither he was going or what the purpose of his life was, or whether at a given moment he was near to or far from its true goal. Is not this symbolic journeying true to human life? Until one's eyes eventually are opened to the whole plan of it, who shall say whether this or that event in our personal life-experience drew us nearer to or farther from the goal we are all unwittingly seeking?

But these ignorant wanderings in a circle, these buffetings of fortune and the tests of character they constitute, at last terminate, and the moment comes when the Prodigal Son at last turns homewards and heads definitely away from the West to the East. His steps may still continue to be irregular; but no matter – they are in the right direction. Intellectually and emotionally he may still tack and wobble from side to side before he attains stable foothold and finds the straight way of peace; but where there's a will there's a way, and he who is bent on finding the way to the East at all costs will assuredly arrive there, and he will arrive bearing within his own character those certificates of fitness for higher things which are implied by the S.W. presenting the Candidate to the W.M. as a fit and proper person and properly prepared to be made a Mason.

6. – The Obligation

Following the traditional practice of the Mysteries and of all secret and monastic Orders, a vow of silence and secrecy is next required from the Candidate as a further preliminary to the conferment of Initiation and the entrustment with any secret information.

This Obligation is often thought of as merely perpetuating the usual covenant of secrecy required by new members of the old Trade Guilds, as a guard to the privileges of the Guild and the protection of technical trade secrets. But whilst the Speculative Craft certainly follows the Operatives in this and other respects, the reasons for secrecy and for being solemnly obligated to it run much deeper than the need for silence about the formal secrets of the Order.

The main purpose of the Obligation is to impress the beginner upon the path of Light and self-knowledge with a sense of the extreme value of silence about the new perceptions that will come to him, the new ideas and experiences he will encounter, and the mental reactions he will experience as the result of them. And it must be emphasised that silence and secrecy are imposed not so much in the interest of the Fraternity at large (which could suffer little from his indiscretions) as in that of the individual Brother himself. Experience will teach him, later on, the deep personal value of silence. He will find that Light and Wisdom are acquired not from anything that can be ocularly shown or orally imparted to him, but from the gradual assembly of new ideas and their gradual digestion and co-ordination by his own mind, for which purpose it is above all things essential that his mental energies should be conserved, not frittered away in talk. To use an electrical analogy, he must become an "accumulator", receiving new impressions and letting them revolve in the closed circle of his own mind, which will gradually digest them and extract their final values.

In the world without the Lodge an appalling waste of human energy occurs daily in the form of needless private chatter and public utterance, which might be re-directed to higher ends. The way of the inner life, upon which one symbolically enters on passing the door of the Lodge, is the reverse. It calls for silence and economy of speech. It remembers one's moral accountability for each spoken word. And, because it calls for the conservation of one's verbal energies and prohibits their needless diffusion in frothy exuberance, it leads by deep and still waters of knowledge, and silence generates the power needed for speaking with authority and effect when the time for such speaking comes.

Turn now to the V.S.L, the Mason's supreme light in these matters. It declares "There is a time to be silent and a time to speak", (Ecclesiastes III: 7). Note that the time for silence comes first in order; for indeed it is not possible to "speak" at all in the high sense here implied until, by a previous discipline of silence, one has acquired the wisdom to know what to say, how, when, and to whom to say it, and is possessed of the spiritual momentum which transforms ordinary speech into winged "words of power". Only after a long discipline of silence is it that "out of the fullness of the heart the mouth speaketh".

It is common with newly made Brethren in the first flush of their new Masonic life to find hosts of new perceptions and ideas welling up in their minds as the result of Initiation and of the thoughts and studies to which their Initiation has led them. To these they feel impelled to give expression, and to teach and share with others things they are just beginning to learn themselves. It is always satisfactory to find that the forces of Initiation have proved effective in them and have kindled their inner fire even to that extent; but it is precisely to the curbing of this crude enthusiasm that the Obligation is largely directed when it ordains silence, and that we owe the traditional practice of restricting the giving of instruction in Masonic science to those who have become Masters of it, and for whom the "time to speak" has come.

For peril attaches to premature and unwise speech no less than to more flagrant violations of secrecy; a peril pointed to in the penalty of the Obligation. That penalty (when we discern the spiritual intention behind the literal expression of it) implies that he who is unfaithful to his duty of silence and secrecy may come to lose the power of effective speech altogether. By frittering away energies which need to be conserved and consolidated he may automatically render himself spiritually unvocal. Says a wise old counsel:

Word is thrall but Thought makes free;
Hold thy speech, I counsel thee.

Observe this further point. The Candidate takes the Obligation upon the visible emblem of the ever-speaking Divine Word (than which nothing is more continually speaking yet nothing is more silent), and by a manual act attaches himself to and indentifies himself with it. By emulating its silence he may eventually recover that Lost Word for which Masonry is the search, and become able to sound it forth through his own person.

A word upon the posture observed during the Obligation, and compare it with what has previously been said about the partial measure of symbolical disrobing the Candidate undergoes in this Degree. Remember also the changing and progressive nature of both the posture and the measure of disrobement adopted during the three Degrees, for they are deeply significant. They imply that, before the aspirant can attain a new regenerate self, his old selfhood must become broken down, its pride humbled, its attachment to external possessions and ingrained mental prejudices severed.

All which is not the work of a moment but a gradual process. He is, therefore, not called upon to do anything beyond his immediate powers, but to follow the principle of "precept upon precept; line upon line; here a little and there a little". Hence it is that the posture (and the unclothing) change in each Degree and affect different limbs and parts of the Candidate's person. In the First Degree only one knee rests on the ground; in the Second it will be the other knee that will mark his progressive humility; whilst in the Third the posture will signify that his humility is no longer partial but total, and that all resistance of mind and stubbornness of will have at last sunk to complete self-surrender to the Good Law upon whose symbolic volume he places first one hand and finally both.

7. – The Restoration to Light

The Candidate is next reminded that for a considerable time he has been in a state of darkness.

Let no one be so literally minded as to imagine that this naïve and simple phrase alludes merely to the few minutes during which the Candidate's sight has been shut off for symbolic reasons. Remember that the whole ceremony is allegory, a parable of the soul's life; that it dramatises in small "the entry of all men upon this their mortal existence"; and that the entirety of that existence has hitherto been spent in a state of darkness and blindness and will so continue to be spent until that spiritual consciousness is regained which we call "Light".

"Our birth is but a sleep and a forgetting," says the poet. Our rebirth, he might have added, is an awakening and a remembering; but it comes about only when there is kindled within us that latent central "Light", to seek which is the purpose of our entrance into this world and to find which is really the predominant wish of every human heart, whether that wish becomes a definite conscious urge or remains dormant and subconscious.

In every Candidate that wish is presumed to have become a definite conscious urge, and because it has become so predominant and overpowering in him that he is without peace of soul until he finds what he has been blindly seeking, he is, by the law of life itself, entitled to have his prayer answered, to have the door opened to his own knocking, and to hear spoken over him the fiat of his own re-creation, "Let there be Light".

Throughout our Ritual by "Light" we must understand "consciousness". "Let there be Light" implies, therefore, "let there be a quickening, heightening and expansion of consciousness in that which has hitherto been unconscious, or but limitedly conscious."

Some measure of consciousness is present in everything, in every kingdom of Nature, from mineral to man. In man is gathered up the consciousness of all the sub-human kingdoms, and in him that consciousness is capable of being advanced still farther; indeed, to a stage beyond the human.

Our First Degree, therefore, implies the first stage of an expansion of consciousness beyond that of the normal mentality. The Second Degree implies a still farther advancement; the Third implies a "raising" to a still higher one; whilst the Supreme Degree of the Royal Arch points to a final sublime "exaltation" of consciousness to which the prior Craft Degrees lead up.

Throughout the sequence of grades is implied a progressive advance from the normal natural mentality to the heights of spiritual consciousness, an advance which is biblically spoken of as "ascending the Hill of the Lord". And each of our Masonic ceremonies has been designed to promote a grade in that ascent.

How far that ascent will be promoted by a particular ceremony, how far a Candidate's conscience may be thereby quickened and expanded, depends upon a combination of three conditions:
- (1) The help of God;
- (2) The preparedness of the Candidate;
- (3) The efficiency of the Lodge and the Initiating Master as instruments for bringing the two former into union.

It need not be supposed that an actual accession of spiritual consciousness to the Candidate comes about instantly and simultaneously with the symbolic act of restoration to light. It may or may not do so. Usually new consciousness emerges but slowly through the darkness of our clouded understanding. To use Masonic analogy, the Sun at the centre of our personal system only mounts to the meridian gradually; there is first a dawn and a gradual rising and a scattering of the darkness before its light manifests in fullness and strength at high noon.

Significance, of course, attaches to the symbolic "firing" in which all present engage at the moment of restoration to light. It is, as it were, a discharge or liberation of the tension to which the assembly has been subjected during the ceremony; it is the outward expression of their co-operation with the Initiating Master in bringing the Candidate from darkness to light; whilst to the Candidate himself it should mean the sound of the breaking of his inward fetters, resulting in that uplifting of soul and sudden access of vision which enables him to say "Whereas before I was blind, now I see!"

SUMMARY OF PART I

The Restoration to Light, the climax and peak-point of the Ceremony, concludes that first portion of it, that series of seven ascending steps of the mystical Mountain, which are associated with his "state of darkness". The remainder of the Ceremony, a series of seven descending steps, occurs in the newly won "state of light", and is devoted to imparting information and instruction in regard to conserving, nourishing and developing that Light within oneself, now that it has once been glimpsed.

Before passing on to this, let us summarise what has preceded. The Ceremony has dramatised in symbolic, swiftly-moving, but comprehensive ritual-form the path to be followed by any one who, under the stress of his own deepest heart-impulses, turns in discontent from the interests of the natural world without, in quest of those of the world within. It explains his own nature and his own past life to him; it indicates the conditions and terms upon which a re-orientation of himself and the satisfaction of his hopes are possible to him; it shows that he must empty himself of his old self, divesting and detaching himself from his past acquisitions, whether intellectual or material. These – his "personal comforts" – will, like those literal ones of the Candidate's, all be restored to him later on, but what new values will they then take on! how amplified and multiplied will their value become to him who, like Job, has consented to be stripped of them that he may find a higher good! To which end, further, he must make a great adventure of faith, letting all go, surrendering himself to invisible guidance, maintaining a resolute will to find what he seeks, breaking down all opposition and interference between himself and his goal, and dedicating himself to the source of Light and to becoming – as a light-bearer himself – an instrument for forms of human service higher than he could ever render without it.

Such is the path of real Initiation as marked out in this Ceremony. It involves blinding the eyes, baring the heart, and tyling the mind to things external and shadowy, that they may open again upon things internal and substantial in a true Restoration to Light.

Then comes the Sun's Light to our hut
When fast the senses' door is shut.
For such a pure and perfect guest
The emptiest room is furnished best.

If the Ceremony does not mean all this, it means nothing worthy of pursuing and is but a vain tradition and formality. If it means all this, but is performed without understanding and without transplanting its implications into our life-conduct, we profane it, increase our own darkness, and act no differently from those who turn mechanical praying-wheels. But if the dispersion of our natural darkness and the rising into consciousness above it of that Sun which glows at the centre of every man's personal system be what we look for, then in our Ceremony surely we have in our hands a means of grace of the first value and efficacy.

PART II

8. – The Revelation of the Greater and the Lesser Lights

It is impossible to formulate in words the condition resulting from actual "restoration to Light". Psychological states are indescribable and must be experienced before they can be understood. But an analogy may help us to an understanding of the enlargement of consciousness which real Initiation effects; for the re-birth of one's mind and spiritual nature (which, as we have said, is implied by Initiation) stands in exact correspondence with, and follows the same law and process as physical birth; the process of "birth" is repeated upon a higher level of the spiral of creation.

Now when a child is born into this world physically, it, as it were, undergoes an initiation into a new state of existence and attains a consciousness which it never previously experienced, and it requires some considerable time before its consciousness becomes adjusted to its new environment, and its vision duly focussed upon objects around it. It is only conscious vaguely and incoherently; time and practice are requisite before it can accustom itself and its eyesight to its surroundings.

Similarly with psychological rebirth. Individual experience of it varies, but broadly one passes into a state of awareness of something having happened in oneself of an expanding and illuminating character. One cannot tell oneself, let alone others, what it is; one merely knows that there has been an upheaval from within, a shifting of one's focus of consciousness from a lower to a higher level, entailing a feeling of liberation from former mental limitations, the promise of much wider mental vision and deeper understanding for the future, and withal a sense of deep, uplifting, but inexplicable happiness. Such is a very crude description of what a duly prepared and responsive Candidate is likely to experience as the result of his Initiation: possibly, but not necessarily, during the conferment of the ceremony, but at some less or greater interval after it. He is, in biblical language, one of those who having, previously sat in darkness, has now suddenly seen a great light, but cannot yet say what that light is or involves, or define any detailed perceptions. All he knows is that he has "received his sight", and that, whereas before he was relatively blind, he is now at last beginning to see.

Now, it will be a very promising fact if the Candidate's Initiation result is a "restoration to light" to the extent just mentioned. For it means that subsequent reflection upon his new experience will steady his quickened emotions and facilitate the adjustment of his mental sight until it is able to attain clear, precise vision of certain truths, just as an infant learns to adjust to objects around it.

Then certain great primary truths of life will gradually emerge and become revealed to him. And those great primary truths are, in our Ceremony, symbolically figured forth in what we call our "Three Great **but Emblematic** Lights". These emblems are actually revealed to the Candidate by the Master as the first objects upon which his eyes look after being given light, and the Candidate is appropriately kept in a kneeling posture, and facing the East, whilst they are exhibited and briefly explained; for how should one contemplate primary fundamental Divine truths save in an attitude of humility and upon one's mental knees? It is very fitting, therefore, that the Three Great Lights should be the **first** objects of the Candidate's perception, and that they should be revealed to him whilst facing East, and whilst in a kneeling posture.

Of what, now, are these Three Great Lights the emblems? They consist, observe, of the V.S.L., the S., and the C.; the three being always displayed as if they were organically and indissociably combined, the V.S.L. lying undermost and forming the base for the other two which rest on it, the C. being partially concealed by the S.

These three emblems we may interpret thus:
  (1) The V.S.L., although embodying the Divine Law as revealed to the Western world, has a far wider significance. For us Masons, it is the visible emblem of the invisible Cosmic Law, through which Deity is manifested in the Universe. It virtually, therefore, represents God Himself who, as Law, underlies everything, and is the basis of all being. "Law" has many forms or modes, and we must, therefore, not limit our ideas of it to any one of them, but rather think of it as comprising them all, as physical law, intellectual law, moral law, and as unifying the dual qualities of Justice and Mercy, of Severity and Love, which characterise the Divine Nature.
  So broad is the Craft's conception of the "Sacred Law" that Masons are not committed to treating the Bible as the only expression of it. Accordingly, the Holy Scriptures of any religion are permitted to be exposed in the Lodge in substitution for the Bible; the principle adopted being that a Candidate may be obligated upon the particular revelation of Cosmic Law which he recognises as true for himself and binding upon his conscience. Thus in many Lodges where men of non-Christian faith are admitted, alternative sets of Scriptures are kept, so that a Jew may be obligated upon the Pentateuch, a Moslem upon the Koran, an Indian upon the Vedas or Puranas, and so on.
  (2) The Compasses resting upon the V.S.L. represent the Divine Spirit or Divine Principle issuing forth from Deity into manifestation, both cosmically and in the individual, and proceeding to function in accordance with the Divine Law.
  (3) The Square set opposite to, but inextricably conjoined with, the Compasses, represents the sheath or vesture of cosmic Matter, in which the Divine Spirit takes form and proceeds to function.

Read in conjunction, then, the Three Great Lights reveal the Cosmic Purpose: i.e. Spirit and Matter working in unison and according to Divine Law to realise an idea or intention latent in the Divine Mind.

What is that Divine Idea? It is that of constructing a perfect Universe, occupied by perfect beings: a Universe in which the animating Spirit and the material form shall stand in perfect balance and, being made in the Divine image and likeness, shall be a perfect expression of the Divine Thought and a fitting tabernacle for the Deity to indwell.

Masonically, we speak of Deity as the Great Architect, and of the Universe as the Cosmic Temple in process of being built in accordance with the Divine Law and Order and with the help of the Divine Compasses and Square; and it is this idea, as being the basis of Masonic doctrine and philosophy, which is, therefore, the first "secret" revealed to every Candidate and displayed to him under the guise of our Triune Great Lights; for, as a Mason, it becomes his duty to co-operate with the Great Architect in executing His plan and erecting the Great Cosmic Temple.

Having been shown the Three Great Lights (or, as we may call them, the three great Cosmic Principles), the Candidate is now turned round from facing the E., and shown Three Lesser Lights burning in different parts of the Lodge. Now these Three Lesser Lights stand in direct correspondence with the three great ones. They are meant to indicate to the Candidate that the three great Cosmic Principles or Lights which sublie the Universe, are reproduced and present in miniature **within himself.** The Universe is the Macrocosm (or **great** image of the Divine Thought); he himself is the Microcosm (or image **in small** of the same Thought), and in him too reside three "lights" enabling him to co-operate with the Great Architect's plan. To him, too, have been entrusted the Compasses of the discerning Mind to direct his own personal life; the Square of bodily form which it will be his task to work into due shape and make meet as a living stone for the Cosmic Temple; whilst the Master Light of Conscience also resides imperishably within him to indicate to him the path of duty.

By the assistance of these Three Lesser Lights the Candidate is enabled (as the Lecture of the Degree will teach him) to perceive for the first time the form of the Lodge; to behold its arrangement, its furniture and jewels, to contemplate its length, breadth and height, the disposition of the Brethren round its sides, whilst its middle portion is left as empty space and illumined by the "Glory in the Centre". Translating this into personal significance, he is meant to realise that all this external imagery is but a picture of himself, seen from within himself and no longer from without. For just as he is now within the Lodge, and able to see what was previously closed to him, so now by the help of his own inner lights he may hope to become able to enter within himself, to contemplate introspectively the spaciousness of his own soul, to observe with what graces and jewels of character he must furnish and adorn it, and to perceive his own personal faculties at the circumference and the presence of that bright Star which blazes at his own centre.

To sum up: the instruction in the Great Lights is to reveal to the Candidate the basic Law and Principles of all being; whilst that in the lesser ones constitutes his first lesson in the "knowledge of himself" and teaches him that those Principles exist also within his own soul and provide him with lights sufficient to shape it into perfection and bring himself into harmony with Cosmic Law.

In the concealment of the lower points of the C. beneath the S. lies a most instructive lesson. Thereby is implied that man's immortal and powerful spirit (represented by the C.) is at present overlain and prevented from full function by the contrary tendencies of his mortal material body, represented by the S.) Now this position must become reversed. If man is to become perfected and rise to the full height and possibilities of his being, his spiritual principle must not remain subordinated to the flesh and its tendencies, but gain ascendancy over them. This the Mason is taught to achieve for himself, and in proportion as he subdues his lower nature he will liberate the powers and faculties of his immortal spirit and rise to mastership over all that is fleshly and material in himself. In the subsequent Degrees this triumph of the spirit over the body will be symbolically evidenced by the points of the C. being progressively raised above the S, first one and then the other, until the Candidate for perfection becomes at last "able to work with both those points and render the circle of his Masonic conduct complete".

9. – The Entrustment with the Secrets

Next follows the Candidate's entrustment with the "secrets" of the Degree. This, however, is preceded by an explanation to him of certain dangers which, unknown to himself, he is told he has already passed, and he is shown the sword and the cabletow. These, of course, are but visible symbols of certain subjective spiritual perils incident to rashly embarking upon the path of spiritual experience and to the moral suicide involved in receding from that path when one's eyes have been opened to it. To the novice these perils are imperceptible, and will not become apparent until after considerable experience; meanwhile he should accept the warning as a wise counsel from those more advanced than himself.

As to the sword that is shown him, let him reflect upon the frequent Scriptural references to the two-edged "sword of the Spirit", to its penetrating power and the way in which it is said to guard access to the central "Tree of Life". This will help him to understand the use of the sword in the Ceremony, and why, on his first entrance to the Lodge, he is made to feel its sharp point.

To the cabletow attaches very considerable significance; indeed, so important is this item of equipment that it appears in one guise (or disguise) or another in each of the three Degrees, as also in the Royal Arch. It is not expedient that its deeper meanings should be spoken about promiscuously even among Masons; like many other things in the Craft, those meanings will either disclose themselves to advancing experience or be imparted privately by a teacher to approved pupils. It may be said, however, that biblically, the cabletow is referred to in the familiar phrase "or ever the **Silver Cord** is loosed" (Ecclesiastes XII: 6) and whoever understands that phrase will perceive why "cord" is used in each of our Ceremonies.

The "secrets" (or arcane truths) imparted in this Degree are explained as consisting of certain peculiar marks or signs, intended to distinguish all Brethren of the elementary grade of Apprentice. Outwardly, in this and in subsequent Degrees also, they are expressed by step, sign and word. These, of course, are not the full or real secrets, but only figurative emblems of them. It is what they signify that constitutes the secrets, and that significance is left for the Candidate to meditate upon and reduce into daily personal practice. Only so will he really learn them and come to understand why they are called "secrets" and why we insist upon their use. They can never be orally communicated, except in symbolic form, but must be learned by experimental practice. Just as a prosperous businessman can never convey the "secret" of his success to someone who has not himself practised it, so the secrets of Masonic progress are learned only by those who actually live them. They are **clues** to spiritual progress rather than confidential communications of secret information.

In being given the formal symbolic secrets the Candidate should reflect that he is receiving a first lesson in a long course of instruction of a private and occult nature: i.e., one not taught outside the Lodge, but hidden from public knowledge and intended to help him upon the path of his personal inner life. For, having but just entered upon that path, it is proper that he should now be instructed how to tread it. He has a long journey to take to reach the goal the Craft opens to him, a goal not yet visible. Hence he should absorb instruction slowly, proceed warily, understandingly, and withal humbly. He has been given a first far-off glimpse of the Light he seeks, but that Light would only confound and blind him were it revealed to him in its fullness, suddenly and abruptly. In his quest of it he should apply to himself the well-worn words of Newman's hymn, "I do not ask to see the **distant** scene; one step enough for me." And it is one step, and only one step at a time, that the Craft permits and teaches in each of our Degrees. Let him see that he carries into daily life all that that one step signifies, for until he has taken it in actual living he will be incapable of taking the subsequent ones. And to the Apprentice Mason seven years are allocated to taking it, though (as the Lecture states) less will suffice if he be found worthy of preferment.

Why so long a period as seven years? The answer lies in the fact that the First Degree of spiritual and Masonic life is one of purification of body and mind in preparation for the attainment of

Light in all its fullness. The unpurified natural man can never reach that Light; his own inherent impurities and darkness will always clog his mind and keep him self-hoodwinked from it. Therefore, purification is necessary and the elimination of everything in him that clouds his vision and coarsens his nature. This takes time. We know our bodies undergo change every seven years. Physiologists declare that during that period every cell and tissue of us undergoes renewal. The man who understands himself and resolutely sets about the work of regeneration can, therefore, rely on Nature's assistance in enabling him within seven years gradually to work off his own impurities and replace them with new material, thus building a cleaner, purer body for himself, one better fitted for being suffused by the Light resident at his own centre. This "septenary law" – one of the key secrets for interpreting life – was well known to the Initiates of old, and it is for this reason that seven years are allotted to the work of the First Degree.

There is much to be learned about the "word" of the Degree and the posture in which it is imparted, but this again must be left to private oral tuition. The directions about the Candidate being "expected to stand perfectly erect", and the references to "right (i.e., straight) lines and angles" and "well-squared actions" comprise a wealth of allusion to secret truths into which the average Brother never thinks it worth while to inquire. To the experienced, however, such matters as bodily posture and the "well-squaring" of one's personal actions (even in such minute matters as writing legibly and with every letter well-formed) have both a physiological and a character value of great importance in relation to the effort to attain spiritual perfection. Nature has had a purpose in slowly raising man's animal body from a horizontal to an erect posture and in transforming his animal instincts and passions into moral rectitude, and she has still further purposes to disclose as resulting from physiological erectness. "Unto the upright ariseth light in the darkness," says the Psalmist; and to Initiates this is literally true. It is a part of their training and discipline to adopt a physically erect posture of the spinal column when engaged in their devotions and meditations, that pillar-like posture being known to be conducive to the attainment of spiritual consciousness or "light". Hence all prayers in the Lodge are said with the Brethren upstanding, for which reason the Masonic Candidate is instructed to "stand perfectly erect" at the moment when the light of the "word" is communicated to him. In former times, for well-understood psycho-physiological reasons, a deformed or diseased person was never accepted as a fit and proper Candidate for Initiation.

As to the "Word" given to the Candidate, a brief hint may be given here. It is said to denote Strength; a better rendering would be Power, Energy, Ardour, all of which are implied by it. It refers to the energy and ardour with which the Candidate should pursue his work of self-perfecting now that he has once begun it; and the word is given him because keenness and energy will prove one of the key-secrets of his successful progress. All creative work depends upon two interacting active and passive forces, energy and resistance, labour and rest. (In the Creation, God first laboured and then rested). The Ceremony reminds us that these two forces were represented at the forefront of Solomon's symbolic temple by two "pillars": i.e., foundation principles. And it is these two principles — activity and contemplation — that the Candidate must learn to apply to himself in rebuilding his own personal temple.

10. – The Testing by the Wardens

Following the entrustment with the Secrets, the Candidate is directed to be led to each Warden in turn and told to communicate them to him. Why is this? It is to ascertain whether he retains the instructions and impressions already communicated to him and can reproduce them, or whether he will fail in so doing, or will pervert or falsify them. In a word he is subjected to a test of his own capacity to retain and live up to what has already been imparted to him.

This episode not only perpetuates the practice of the Ancient Mysteries but is entirely accordant with Scriptural authority and with spiritual experience. For it is a fact, indeed a law, of life that no one receives an accession of knowledge or power or even of material wealth without being soon afterwards put to a test as to how he will use it and whether he is able and worthy to retain it. If he is, he will be still further advanced; not, he will remain where he was or be degraded to a worse position than at first. "To him that hath shall be given; and from him that hath not shall be taken away even that which he hath." Remember to what a severe testing Job was subjected after acquiring great wealth; remember, too, the "temptation" or testing episode related in the Gospels as occurring to Jesus immediately after his accession of spiritual light at the Jordan baptism.

And so it will be to everyone for whom our Initiation Ceremony becomes translated into terms of actual life-experience. As soon as Light or Wisdom has been vouchsafed him, he will find himself tested in one or another way as to his worthiness to receive it. "He who has not been tested **knows** nothing" says a wise Master (Thomas à Kempis), for no new truth can become one's own until it has been reduced to personal conduct and lived out under the stress of opposition and temptation to the contrary.

Earlier in our Ceremony, you will remember, the Candidate was conducted to the Wardens in turn and, arousing them from silence, provoked them to speak to him; and it was explained that in doing so the Candidate was symbolically calling into activity certain higher forces latent in himself but previously dormant. It is those same latent forces or higher principles in himself that will put him to the test now that his intelligence has been accorded a certain small measure of Light. Can he retain that Light? Does he still exhibit the "sign" of a true Mason? Is he still striving to tread the path and to take the "step"? Does he remember and act upon the "word" that was given him? Does his daily life show that he is uttering that word – if not in its completeness, at least in broken syllables or letters? (Our practice of "halving" or "lettering" the word is not merely for precautionary reasons or to show that we share its secret with other Brethren, but as a most instructive and delicate reminder that, though we be unable to utter that word in its entirety, yet if we can only sound it forth in stumbling but sincere fragmentary efforts, those fragments will suffice to let us pass our test).

If, therefore, we pass the test, we are permitted and directed to pass on to higher attainments, and it is of this that the sending round of the Candidate to the Wardens to prove himself a Mason is a dramatic and symbolic representation.

11. – The Investiture with the Apron

Since each episode in the Ceremony follows its predecessor with far-seeing wisdom and psychological accuracy, we shall now see how great and fitting a reward awaits the Candidate as the result of passing the test to which he has just been submitted.

On the S.W. reporting to the Master that the Candidate has made real and demonstrable progress in the science, the Master forthwith gives directions for the investment with the Apron. Thereupon, for the first time the Candidate becomes Masonically clothed and entitled thenceforth to wear the glorious badge of the Order.

Behind this act of investment lies an important but ultra-physical truth, namely, that every spiritual state into which the human soul passes is accompanied by an appropriate bodily form.

The ancient maxim of the Initiates about this is "*Nullus spiritus sine indumento*"; no spirit (or spiritual condition) exists without possessing its appropriate form or garment; or, in Scriptural words, "God giveth it a body as it pleaseth Him, and to every seed (or soul) its own body". And accordingly, on the Candidate being certified as having attained a new phase of soul-growth, the Master (as the Divine representative in the Lodge) at once orders him to be clothed upon with a vesture expressive of his spiritual condition.

How fitting a vesture the Apron is will appear on perceiving its emblematic value. It is at once one of the most important and comprehensive of our symbols. Its shape is that of an equilateral triangle, superimposed upon a quadrangle whose sides are equal also. The triangle is the primitive and universal emblem of what really is Spiritual and Formless, whilst the quadrangle is that of what is Material and possesses Form (or body); and, since human nature is a compound of both, the Apron is a figure of man himself. And because the triangle and quadrangle are among the most ancient ideographs in the world, and indeed as old as humanity itself, the Apron is very truly described as being "a badge older than that of any other Order in existence".

The Apron is also of white lambskin; an emblem, therefore, of purity, of innocence and infancy; an appropriate clothing for one just born into the Masonic life. It is five-pointed, in allusion to man's five-sensed nature and to many other occult truths concerning humanity. If you add the three sides of its triangular part to the four of its quadrangular, you get seven, the number of completeness in Nature, corresponding with the septenary of colours in the spectrum, the notes of the musical scale, and the days of the week. If you multiply them, you get twelve, the cosmic number, comprising the twelve Zodiacal Signs through which our Solar System moves and which are reflected in the twelve Hebrew Tribes and the twelve Apostles.

As the Candidate advances through the Degrees and perhaps eventually becomes advanced to the higher sections of the Masonic Hierarchy, he will find at each new step a corresponding change in the form and colours of his Apron. It will manifest what are known as the sacred or royal colours – blue, purple and scarlet – whilst to its unadorned simplicity will be added ornamentations of the precious metals, at first silver and afterwards gold. These elaborations of the Apron are meant to symbolise corresponding progress in him who wears it, and point to the unfolding of spiritual graces and powers from the depths of his own inward being. As the strength of his central spirit grows, so his Apron will burgeon forth in symbolic rosettes and become decorated with celestial blue and ornaments of silver; and, as it intensifies still further, the pale azure will deepen correspondingly to royal blue, and silver will be displaced by gold – the emblem of wisdom and spiritual royalty. The Apron, moreover, is attached to the body by a fastener in the form of a serpent – the emblem of Wisdom, to indicate the wisdom with which his whole organism has been devised.

Let the Candidate, then, see in the Apron a symbol of himself and, in its progressive beautifying, reflect that it calls for the manifestation of corresponding growth of spirituality in his own life. Let him regard his Apron with a respect comparable to that with which he should regard his own soul, keeping it, so far as may be, sacred and undented, never treating it with levity nor entrusting it to any hands but his own. For, being the symbol of himself, it should be respected as the outward and visible image of his inward invisible self.

As it is written that no man may enter heaven without wearing a "wedding garment" (i.e., a vesture qualifying him for union with the celestial life), so no Mason may enter a Lodge without wearing the Apron that proclaims his fellowship and amity with the universal Craft. But we need not restrict our thought or even our use of the Apron to wearing it in Lodge; it is helpful to imagine ourselves as clothed with it at all times, whether we are actually wearing it or not. There are some Brethren who gird on their Masonic clothing in private, ere engaging in their personal devotions. And there are some who, loyal to its meaning in their lifetime, like still to wear their Apron in the grave.

12. – The Charge in the N.E. Corner

Clothed upon Masonically, the Candidate is then placed in the N.E. corner of the Lodge. By "the Lodge" was formerly meant not the room in which the Ceremony takes place, but the Lodge-board or Trestle-board, now called the Tracing-board, to the N.E. corner of which the Candidate's feet were angulated; a practice still obtaining in some Lodges and one that seems desirable to pursue.

The N.E. corner is a point of much symbolic significance. It is the meeting place of N. and E., of darkness and light, and, therefore, representative of the Candidate's own condition. Standing at this point, he can henceforward at will step onward to the E., or backward to the N., advancing further to the Light or relapsing into darkness; it will rest with himself which direction his life will henceforth take.

He is charged, however, to make his present position the basis of renewed spiritual activity and to regard his personality as a "foundation-stone", now well and truly laid, as the material for raising thereon a "super-structure". By this expression is meant something much more than mere character-building, as it is often thought to mean. What is implied may perhaps be gathered by reference to some of the older Masonic rituals in which instead of "super-structure", the Candidate is told to build a "castle in the air", an expression which, far from meaning something dreamy and imaginary as it popularly has come to do, really refers to an "airy", ethereal or spiritual body, "a house not made with hands nor subject to decay [like his temporal body] but eternal and heavenly".

This leads one into deeper metaphysics than can be dealt with here, and the subject must be left to private reflection and tuition, with merely the hint that, as our mortal visible body has been built up gradually, cell by cell and tissue by tissue, out of the essences and life forces of temporal Nature, so Man has within him the capacity to raise thereupon, and to evolve from himself, an immortal invisible "super-structure", an "airy" castle or fortress into which his conscious soul will retreat and clothe itself when its earthly vesture falls away. The erection of the super-structure is known in Masonic mysticism as the "building King Solomon's Temple", which every Mason must build for himself.

A further subject upon which the Candidate is charged in the N.E. corner is the duty of Charity, the complete attainment of which is elsewhere spoken of as the summit of the Mason's profession. Now, it is idle to think of this virtue and its attainment as being fulfilled by money donations to those who are financially poor, distressed or deserving. The usual words of the Ritual may suggest that it does, but remember that the Ritual throughout is a veil, and always masks far deeper truths than its surface words exhibit.

The "Charity" the Candidate is so earnestly entreated to cultivate at this important moment and throughout his subsequent life would perhaps be best interpreted by the word "compassion" – universal compassion for, and sympathetic feeling with, all living creatures, human and sub-human. Such a definition includes Love, which is the usual synonym for Charity, but it embraces even something more. "Charity", in its Latin original *Caritas*, means "dearness", and the Masonic virtue and duty is that of regarding all creatures in a spirit of universal and impartial **dearness**, as being all pilgrims upon a single path and, whilst in differing degrees of development, yet all evolving towards a common goal. In their struggles and sufferings to work out that destiny, which is theirs no less than yours, and whether they are conscious of that destiny or not, and whether they will thank you for your help or not, it is nevertheless the Mason's duty to give them all the compassion and help he can. Giving what is personal and material is the lowest, and not always a wise, form of giving. Giving mental and moral succour is relief of far greater value, because it braces the mental and moral nature of the recipients. Giving oneself from the heart in a constant sacrificial outpouring of the spirit may yield no **visible** result but is yet the highest of all forms of giving, and it is this which the Mason is counselled to practice, since what he radiates will quicken the life of all around him and send forth leaves from his own tree of life for the healing of the nations. At the Centre of each man's personal system dwells a sun, clouded though it may now be by the fogs and mists of his own making, which, like the solar orb in Nature, can send forth its generous beneficent radiation persistently, unstintingly, and impartially to the good and the evil alike. All the great teachers and enlighteners of humanity have been suns in that sense and because their lives were based upon compassion for the whole world; and it is for the Initiate to try to emulate them.

Consider the philosophy of giving and why it must needs be more blessed than receiving. Natural man is necessarily selfish, grasping, self-acquisitive. All his days he has been receiving – from Nature, from his parents, from society – and has become egocentric and habituated and trained to securing for himself a living, a position and an individuality. But the Mason is a man who, by the very fact of his seeking Initiation, is impelled by forces within himself to rise beyond Nature and to submit himself to a law higher than that of self-acquisition. All his energies have now to be reversed; getting must give way to giving; centripetal tendencies must become transformed to centrifugal radiation of the highest qualities in him. In Matthew Arnold's words:

Know, man is all that Nature is but more,
And in that "more" lie all his hopes of good.

From that "more" the Mason builds a "super-structure" upon the foundation of his old self; not, as formerly, by a process of getting and receiving but by one of giving forth that others may live. And the more he gives the more he must eventually receive, for all energy is conserved and, like expanding water-ripples, returns upon its source, enriched by every contact it has made in its passage.

Hence it is that the Candidate is charged to learn that self-giving is the foundation-law and foundation-stone of the higher life; that Charity has its degrees and may be practised in many ways and upon different planes, the highest of which is the habitual pouring forth of compassionate love to all beings; that he who has freely received must as freely give; and that as he, by his Initiation, has been given the blessing of light and understanding he never before possessed, so now the Law of life itself requires that, from this moment, he shall never withhold that light from any who asks it from him.

Surely one of the most moving moments of an impressive Ceremony is that in which the Candidate, pauperised and denuded of everything material, is invited to make a gift to his poor and distressed fellow-creatures. Out of what resources can he make it save from treasury of his own heart – without the backing of which no gift, whatever its form, can have any true value? The incident is meant to teach him that if that treasury be empty, how can he really give at all, however opulent he be pecuniarily? – but if it be filled, he will be giving what guineas cannot buy.

13. – The Working Tools

In the N.E. Corner the Candidate is advised **what** to do, what to aim at, in order to promote his own advancement. The next thing is to tell him **how** to do it. He is, therefore, recommended to pursue certain lines of self-discipline and self-improvement, which are referred to under the guise of "working tools".

These working tools are three, and as their mystical significance is sufficiently explained on their presentation to the Candidate it is needless to repeat it here. They must not be looked upon, however, as merely emblems incidental to the Ceremony and thereafter to be ignored or forgotten, but as representing duties essential to Masonic progress and meant to be put to practical daily observance.

One of these three tools, the measuring gauge, is itself threefold in its application. It allocates one's daily time to the performance of three distinct duties, duties not necessarily involving equal expenditure of time, but duties each of which is of equal value. It inculcates:

(1) A duty to God and a persistent devotion to **spiritual** things,
(2) A duty to oneself, involving due attention to **material** pursuits and the care of one's own person, and
(3) An **altruistic** duty to those less happily placed than oneself;

as it were an equilateral triangle of duties each of which is as important as the other two, indeed it will be helpful to think of the sides of such a triangle as signifying God, oneself and one's neighbour respectively, and constituting a unity, a whole of which each part is necessary to the others.

The Mason must find a way of balancing his performance of these three duties, so as to make of them an equilateral and not an unequally-sided triangle. Equal attention is called for to spiritual things, to himself, and to what is other than himself, i.e., his neighbour; undue preponderance in either direction will prevent a true balance. That is why, whilst told to give altruistic help to his neighbour, he is also told that he should not do so "unless he can do it without detriment to himself or connections". At first blush these qualifying words sound selfish, contrary to the spirit of self-sacrifice. But there is great wisdom in them. For only he can really serve and help another who has first discharged his duty to himself and made himself competent to serve. "Self-love [says Shakespeare] is not so vile a sin as self-neglect"; and there are many people who neglect to improve themselves, whilst fussily trying to improve others. But selfishness will itself disappear if devotion be habitually accorded to what is higher than self, and this attainment will then in turn qualify him to help his neighbour.

As the Candidate progresses he will learn of other working tools in the further Degrees, but these he will find himself unable to use unless he has first accustomed himself to those of the First Degree. Therefore, he is counselled to slur nothing over, but to pay attention to even the minutest instructions of the Ritual until they suffuse his life and their performance becomes a habit. He will find his education greatly helped if he will enter upon the systematic reading of literature dealing with Masonic and cognate subjects. "Reading is good prayer" says an old counsel, provided it be of a kind that helps one's quest for Light, and, since Masonry is so largely a work of the mind, every study that conduces to the expansion of his mental faculties will prove a "working tool" and open fresh doors of perception to him.

THE CEREMONY OF INITIATION

14. – The Tracing Board

The concluding instruction to the Candidate is the explanation of the Tracing Board, though for convenience this is often deferred to another occasion, since it is necessarily lengthy.

It will have been observed that the Candidate has already been instructed in certain **spiritual** and **ethical** matters, and there now only remains to supplement these by appealing to his **intellectual** nature. This is done by introducing him to the Tracing Board and imparting to him certain esoteric information of a philosophical character. By "esoteric" is meant information not imparted outside the Lodge or taught by churches and other systems provided for public instruction, but which has always been reserved for more private and advanced tuition and which has been perpetuated in secret and embodied in hieroglyphic or symbolic pictures. At one time these cryptic designs were never exposed to the risk of public gaze, but were drawn upon the floor of the Lodge by the Initiating Master when occasion required and were expunged by the Candidate at the close of the Ceremony. Today they are kept permanently depicted upon the Lodge Board. A detailed examination of the First Degree Tracing Board appears in a previous Lodge Paper, and need not, therefore, be repeated here.

In the official Lecture explaining the Board the new Mason is recommended "to seek a Master and from him gain instruction", once more instancing the truth "Seek and ye shall find". This refers to an age-old practice by which every junior Brother sought out and attached himself for seven years to an expert Master for the purpose of gaining much fuller private tuition in the science than is possible at meetings of the Lodge. The relationship of Master and Apprentice, which obtained in the Trade Guilds and later on became an ordinary business practice, was originally one in which the Master undertook not the commercial but the spiritual training of the neophyte, a practice which obtains throughout the East today and which was always observed in the Mysteries of antiquity. With us the practice has, unfortunately, fallen into desuetude because so few Masters are competent to teach and so few

Candidates are wishful or even ripe to learn what lies beneath the surface of the Craft doctrine.

Where, however, the true relationship of Master and Disciple does exist it becomes an intimate and precious one, involving the forging of a spiritual tie and a reciprocal responsibility, which neither of them would lightly sever. This is a subject about which far more can be said than is possible here, but let us reflect that an old maxim of our science is that "when the pupil is ready the Master will be found waiting", and that such Master will impart personal instruction of a far deeper and wider character than can be given publicly or promiscuously.

Finally, the Candidate is told to retire from the Lodge to be restored to what are called, a little ironically, his "personal comforts" – the poor trappings and belongings he surrendered before entering a place where such possessions have no value. Nevertheless, a pointed lesson lies in his being directed to resume them, for henceforth it will be his duty to recast his estimate of them, and, whilst using them for what they are worth, to learn to discriminate between what is of transient and what is of enduring moment. What he has hitherto deemed and clung to as "comforts" he may find to be irksome discomforts later on, until he acquires that wisdom and balanced understanding which reacts neither to comfort nor discomfort, but looks beyond both.

***

The **Ancient Charge** with which the Ceremony usually concludes is self-explanatory and need not be examined here. Strictly it is not an integral factor of the Ceremony, from which it differs both in method and language. The Ceremony proper is "veiled in allegory" and contains cryptic phrases and sub-surface allusions at every turn, whilst the "Ancient Charge" has no ulterior meaning whatever. It is merely a simple homily complimenting the Candidate upon his reception into the Order and informing him of some observances with which he will be expected to comply.

The Charge obviously embodies advice formerly tendered to young men on becoming apprenticed to the Operative Building Guilds, enjoining them to good citizenship and to leading a moral and useful life. But as present-day Candidates for Speculative Masonry are assumed to hold these qualifications before joining the Craft, the Charge is of interest only as perpetuating an old custom of the Trade Guilds on admitting an Apprentice to membership.

CONCLUSION

Summing up this examination of the Ceremony, then, we see its purpose is as follows. The first half of it designed to restore to Light (in the spiritual sense already explained) a Candidate who seeks Light from his heart and comes prepared in mind and person to receive it. The second and complementary half of it is meant to teach him who has been brought to that Light how to retain it and increase it, so that he may never relapse into his former darkness.

In being initiated, a Candidate is being vouchsafed an initial glimpse into supra-natural Light, but only a first glimpse; it rests with himself to prove worthy of it and to enlarge that temporary glimpse into wider and permanent vision. The Ceremony dramatises, in a few swift episodes and pregnant words, the "Apprentice" stage of the spiritual life; it inculcates that, with increasing self-purification and discipline of his material nature, the light of that spiritual Sun which burns and blazes at his own centre and which has now for the first time appeared above his conscious horizon, will manifest in ever-increasing power. As that Sun rises higher and higher within him, so will his own darkness become correspondingly dispelled, and his materialism spiritualised, and his personality transformed into a translucent vessel. "If thine eye [soul] be single [simple and unadulterated by passion and wrong notions,] thy whole being will be full of Light."

He is taught by that Light to see that the substratum of all things is Divine Law, Law which comprises physical, moral and ultra-physical aspects, and in which the roots of his own being are integrated; and therefore, in proportion as he unifies his personal will with the Universal Will and harmonizes his mind and conduct with their Cosmic Prototype, he must needs become a more perfect expression of them and a conscious collaborator with them. And because Love is the fulfilling of the Law, he is enjoined to cultivate that boundless charity and compassion towards all beings which bears, believes, hopes and endures all things, because it understands the operation of that Law and sees clearly the end to which it is shaping us. *Tout aimer, c'est tout comprendre.*

The Apprentice stage of Masonry is, therefore, one of purification, education and self-control, which every Brother must work out and live out for himself. No amount of book knowledge or instruction from others can teach him what can be learned only from his own experience and effort. Even these notes, lengthy as they are, are but an elementary preface to far deeper aspects of Initiation than can be spoken of openly, yet which any ardent aspirant may come to learn as he proceeds. To tell the fuller truths about the subject would scare and discourage rather than enlighten and help; and for this reason the science is, and always was, a veiled and secret one.

One useful counsel may be added which the Candidate should observe if he wishes to progress. It is, never to measure what he finds within the Lodge by his own opinions or by the same standard of judgment that he applies to things without it. Many Brethren go wrong here by lacking humility and teachableness. They try to look at matters of the inner life with the same eyes as those of the outer life. They reserve their ideas of Masonry till they see how far they can square it with other views and beliefs that they hold, and they seek to apply their worldly wisdom to a wisdom which is hidden and not of this world, and their "common sense" to a subject requiring a special education and the use of a sense which in the present state of human evolution is far from common. But spiritual things must be spiritually discerned, and not from the standpoint of unenlightened opinion and unspiritual perception.

He who enters the Lodge in quest of Light should leave all his previous learning behind him with his garments and loose the shoes of personal opinion from off his feet. He should think of himself as a child, and as being taken into a world of new sights and sounds, and where new ideas and even a different logic obtain from those with which he has previously been familiar, and where he must begin to recast his ideas and his life. Will his pride suffer him to stultify himself to this extent?

If it will not, he will but continue to darken his own light, and the Craft can teach him nothing of value, whatever titular rank he may attain in it. If it will, then he may hope to become an Initiate in fact as well as in name and to find his eyes opening to depth beyond depth of truth of which he is at present unconscious.

In the Mysteries of old the Candidate, because of his new birth into Light, was always spoken of as a "child" or a "little child", and in the Sacred Volume which forms the chief textbook of our science we find how often, and for the same reason, such expressions as "the young man" and "little children" are employed.

It accords little with the modern mental temper to cast aside all one's knowledge and preconceptions and reduce oneself to the docility, the naiveté and single-mindedness of infancy. Yet these qualities still remain indispensable to the Candidate for Wisdom, and it still is not the learned, the critical and the worldly wise, but the "little children" who are suffered to come to the Light and are not forbidden from finding it, for of such are both the Kingdom of Heaven and the Craft of Masonry, which is designed to lead to that Kingdom.

Other books by Robert Lomas

The Lewis Guide to Masonic Symbols
A Miscellany of Masonic Essays
The Lost Key
The Secret Science of Masonic Initiation
The Secret Power of Masonic Symbols
Turning the Hiram Key
Turning the Solomon Key
Turning the Templar Key
The Secrets of Freemasonry

The Man Who Invented the Twentieth Century
The Invisible College
Freemasonry and the Birth of Modern Science

Mastering Your Business Dissertation

Books co-authored by Robert Lomas

With Chris Knight
The Hiram Key
The Second Messiah
Uriel's Machine
The Book of Hiram

With Geoff Lancaster
Forecasting for Sales and Materials Management

Kindle eBooks by Robert Lomas

A Miscellany of Masonic Essays

The Secret Science of Masonic Initiation

Turning the Hiram Key

Turning the Solomon Key

Turning the Templar Key Part 1 – The True Origins of Freemasonry *[This ebook contains the Masonic History sections from Turning the Templar Key with additional information about early Freemasonry.]*

The Secrets of Freemasonry

The Lost Key

W.L. Wilmshurst's *The Ceremony of Initiation* Revisited

The Man Who Invented the Twentieth Century

The Invisible College

Freemasonry and the Birth of Modern Science

Mastering Your Business Dissertation

CPSIA information can be obtained at www.ICGtesting.com
Printed in the USA
LVOW10s2113290114

371501LV00024B/1295/P